# N
RA
5

A Guide to the Privatised Railway

JOHN GLOVER

IAN ALLAN Publishing

First published 1996

ISBN 0 7110 2457 X

Published by Ian Allan Publishing

an imprint of Ian Allan Ltd, Terminal House, Station Approach, Shepperton, Surrey TW17 8AS. Printed by Ian Allan Printing Ltd, Coombelands House, Coombelands Lane, Addlestone, Surrey KT15 1HY.

Title page: Princes Risborough now consists only of the former up platform on the through lines, with a single track section northwards to Bicester. Three-car unit No 165037 departs with the 1845 Marylebone to Birmingham Snow Hill on 19 July 1993. *John Glover*

Front cover: The dual voltage Class 319 units are amongst the most versatile of rolling stock types. Will this become the norm, rather than the exception, for new construction? All are owned by Porterbrook Leasing. One of the Thameslink fleet, 319.057, heads an 8-car formation away from Mitcham Junction on a working to Luton. *John Glover*

Back cover: The concourse at Liverpool Street in the morning peak. *John Glover*

CONTENTS

Introduction

The purpose of this book is to describe the principal changes to the organisation of Britain's railways under the Railways Act 1993.

This was not a minor event, since the Act has spelt the end of the integrated railway system owned and operated by a single body, which was established upon Nationalisation on 1 January 1948. Yet the years since World War 2 can hardly be said to have been an unqualified success for British Railways. Quite why this should have been so is a matter for debate, while a fully successful remedy has so far eluded a succession of governments, of both political complexions. It will be several years before the results of the British Government's recent initiative become fully apparent, even if future circumstances do not force adjustments to their chosen course.

First, some of the key events of the last few years and their dates.

The book starts by considering the background to the changes, which began in earnest with the publication of the Government's White Paper 'New Opportunities for the Railways' on 14 July 1992. One immediate result was that the House of Commons Transport Committee set up an inquiry into 'The Future of the Railways...'; their first report was published on 13 January 1993 and a second, much fuller report, on 20 April 1993. The Railways Bill itself was published on 22 January 1993, and progressed through Parliament in the usual manner.

With limited changes, the Railways Bill became law on 5 November 1993. After a period to allow for the necessary restructuring of the railway, the main provisions came into force on 1 April 1994. Briefly, the most far-reaching changes were perhaps:

- the separation of British Rail's operations from the infrastructure on which the services run, with the infrastructure passing to the ownership of the newly set up company, Railtrack;

- the creation of the post of Director of Rail Franchising, whose duties include the securing of railway passenger services by a series of franchise agreements with private operators;

- the parallel creation of a Rail Regulator, whose duties include the licensing of operations, the approval of operator access agreements with Railtrack and the enforcement of competition law;

- the setting up of three rolling stock companies to own the locomotives and rolling stock, which are then leased to the operating companies; and

- the restructuring of the freight businesses with a view to their subsequent sale.

The Railways Act contains 154 sections and 14 schedules, spread over 244 pages. (By comparison the Transport Act 1947, which nationalised virtually the whole of the inland transport industry in Britain, confined itself to 170 rather smaller pages.) There is, of course, much more to the Railways Act, and various aspects are discussed in successive chapters. Neither is only the Railways Act to be considered, since European legislation, after remaining relatively dormant in the transport sector for several years, is now assuming a more prominent role.

This is a story of which only the initial chapters can as yet be written. It is hoped that the reader will find it of value in getting to grips with what is happening to the railway of the late 1990s.

Finally, whatever misgivings we might have, let us cheer ourselves with s4(1)(b) of the Act. This gives the Rail Regulator the duty 'to promote the use of the railway network in Great Britain for the carriage of passengers and goods, and the development of that railway network, to the greatest extent that he considers economically possible'. And who could argue with that?

Left: **Class 317320 is ready to depart with a local train to Euston as a Freightliner passes through on the down platform at Northampton in May 1989.** John Glover

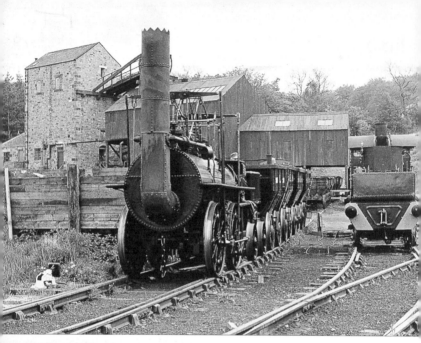

This is how they were described by the historian G. M. Trevelyan, half a century ago. Who would thus describe the railways now? This chapter looks briefly at their formative years to see what lessons might be drawn.

Before railways

The first major transport infrastructure construction in inland Britain was carried out by the Romans. Many of their roads, albeit subsequently improved beyond recognition, remain in use today. But the resources which could be harnessed by invading armies who need to move troops and supplies were not available to the general population and with the Roman withdrawal in AD410, both the need for the roads and the ability to maintain them disappeared; it was well over a thousand years before any serious attention was given to them again.

The Industrial Revolution of the late 18th century marked a decisive change. Factories were built for textile manufacture and iron making, producing industrial towns. They depended first on water power, then on coal power — and hence the establishment of the coal mining industry.

In transport, the whole lived off a combination of inadequate and poorly maintained roads, navigable rivers which were later supplemented by canals, and coastwise shipping. 'Plateways' for metal-wheeled vehicles, albeit horse-drawn, made a slow appearance. It was the coupling of this embryonic technology with the possibilities afforded by the steam engine which allowed the 'Railway Age' to take off.

Above left: **Railways first saw the light of day in the north of England. This working replica of** *Locomotion* **is to be seen at the Beamish Open Air Museum, where it was photographed on 1 June 1984.** *John Glover*

Left: **'The Plant Centenarian' celebrated 100 years of Doncaster Works with a special train hauled by Great Northern Railway Ivatt Atlantics Nos 990** *Henry Oakley* **and 251. The date was 20 November 1953 and the pair are seen here at King's Cross.** *Author's collection*

The railway arrives

The Stockton and Darlington Railway opened in 1825 to transport coal from the Durham coalfield to the River Tees. It did exceedingly well, to the extent that congestion was rife. The authorising Act provided that any person could, by paying the charges, put his own horse and carriage on the railway, and a number of competing services were run simultaneously.

Well, we all learn by experience, don't we? The Parliament of the day had supposed that once free access to the line had been secured for carriers, and the tolls payable by those carriers to the railway company were fixed, free competition would secure the best and cheapest service in the interest of the public.[1]

In concept, however, the Stockton and Darlington was completely overshadowed by the Liverpool & Manchester Railway of 1830. Steam power in the form of Stephenson's *Rocket* unquestionably triumphed, and the railway itself broke decisively with the canal and turnpike business practices. Thus, the Liverpool & Manchester:

● both owned and operated the railway itself;

● forbade its use by outside parties on payment of a toll;

● employed a regular staff, without subcontracting any operations; and

● lifted the scale of investment to a new order of magnitude.

There was a clear emphasis on passenger traffic right from the start, and it carried on average well over 1,000 passengers a day in its first three years of operation. For the 30 miles between the two important commercial cities, trains averaged 20mph. It was a huge improvement on the only passenger alternative, the horse.

Interestingly, Parliamentary papers of 1839 suggested that even if on-line competition were practicable, it was not desirable, since:

'the safety of the public also requires that upon each railway there should be one system of management... On this account it is necessary that the company should possess complete control...although they should therefore acquire an entire monopoly. (Thus) it becomes most important that (the railways themselves) should be so controlled as to secure the public as far as possible from any abuse that might arise.[2]

Shortly afterwards, the Government set up the railway Department in the Board of Trade, under the Railway Regulation Act of 1840. This was the origin of today's Railway Inspectorate.

With the Liverpool & Manchester showing the way, the railway moved into a major role. Its route between two of the country's major cities and in a major industrial area was undoubtedly well chosen, while the consistent 9.5% dividend paid by the L&M to its shareholders was generally admired. The highly competitive technical attributes of railways made system expansion prolific, since the possession of a railway station was clear indication that the locality had 'arrived'.

Thus, the railways grew, fuelling industrial expansion and urban growth in countries around the world. In Britain, though, there was nothing which could even remotely be called centralised planning in railway provision. Development of the network was left entirely to market forces. An Act of Parliament had to be obtained on each occasion, and no little energy was expended in trying to adjudicate between the competing commercial objectives of opposing promoters. But the railways as built, largely in the middle years of the 19th century, were wholly private undertakings.

Evolution

The expansionist years were not without their problems. In a settled land, the interests of landowners had to be considered as well as those of the industrialists who were more likely to provide the traffic. It is accepted nowadays that many landowners were overcompensated in relation to the earning potential of the lines, and that much construction was over-optimistic in relation to the potential benefits. While the railways as a whole

Below: The old Euston was not a place of beauty. LMS Compound 4-4-0 No 40933 heads an arriving train on the east side of the station in the mid-1950s. On the right may be seen a Scammell Scarab, much used at the time for parcels cartage work.
Author's collection

were profitable, this was at the expense of what became excessive cross-subsidisation. Although this could be tolerated under a near monopoly, it was to be a major drawback when real competition later became apparent.

New markets also emerged. City growth led to the separation of homes and employment, and this in turn led to the establishment of the suburban railway. Some railway companies encouraged suburban growth; others considered the traffic as having more of a nuisance value. However, the railways, and later trams and then buses, had a considerable effect on the shape and extent of cities before planning legislation in much more recent times became effective.

Within cities, the problem was if anything worse. The decision not to allow the main line railways into the centre of London (with a few very limited exceptions) made movement within the capital exceedingly difficult. Salvation came with the development of the Underground railway from 1863.

After World War 1 the Government decided that the fragmented state of the main line railways with their plethora of companies would be more economically combined into four major operators. The 'Grouping' into the 'Big Four' companies took effect in 1923. The principal idea was that the inter-company rivalry would be reduced, together with the cost and inefficiency of the duplication of the facilities. But the General Strike and the economic depression of the interwar years was to make the new companies' task an uphill struggle.

A welcome development was the streamline era of the 1930s. Competition took the form of emulation, with the development of high quality express passenger trains on the principal routes. It was the era of 'The Coronation' (LNER) and 'Coronation Scot' (LMS). Steam remained the source of power for railway operations generally, which allowed the locomotive engineers to demonstrate their prowess. Diesel traction was still confined to a handful of shunting locomotives. Electricity had received rather greater exploitation, but mainly for suburban links.

Suburban expansion in the London area was extensive in the interwar years. London Underground extensions, such as the Piccadilly Line to Cockfosters, were financed by cheap loans. On the Southern Railway, a new line was constructed to Chessington South.

For freight traffic, the railway was still a major carrier. The following is gleaned from a contemporary description of the rebuilt Surbiton in 1936:[3]

'Of particular note is the extent to which provision for freight traffic is made. On the south side of the main line are four sidings with a coal wagon capacity of 97, and three sidings for merchandise, capacity 50 wagons. There is also a goods shed. Alongside is a Carter Paterson & Co (carriers) depot. On the north side are sidings for 62 wagons and 14 coaches, also a cattle dock and a milk dock. In the station itself are two parcels offices.'

By this date, road transport was becoming an unwanted competitor, which unlike the railways had no restrictions on its charging policies. It seems incredible nowadays that railway freight rates had both to be determined in advance and applied impartially to all comers. No wonder there was scope for undercutting them. In 1938, the railways launched a demand for a 'Square Deal' to even up the terms of business, but no progress was made with the onset of World War 2.

War and its aftermath

World War 2 put an enormous strain on the railways, from civilian evacuation, through the need for helping the war effort in offence and defence, to troop transport, and food supplies. Most debilitating in the longer term was the enforced inadequacy of maintenance, the lack of new construction, and the effects of enemy damage. The railway is a long-term organisation, and it is just not possible to compensate for such shortcomings quickly.

Nationalisation in 1948 was the response of the postwar Labour Government, with the newly created British Railways placed under the aegis of the British Transport Commission. However, materials were short, as was the political will to give priority to righting the by then extensive shortcomings of the railway system. Road transport was less inhibited and was boosted by the sale of surplus vehicles from the armed services and the end of petrol rationing. The bus industry peaked in 1952/3, and has declined steadily since.

The railway Modernisation Plan appeared in 1955, with a clear aim to restore prewar standards and to make up for the missed years. Large-scale electrification and dieselisation were to replace the steam locomotive, and investment in virtually everything was promised. Sadly, progress was relatively slow, while the financial results were exceedingly doubtful. They attracted withering comment. In 1960, the Permanent Secretary at the Ministry of Transport said that it was difficult to understand 'how the whole of the modernisation scheme could possibly have the economic results forecast by the BTC in their last reappraisal'. In that same year Swindon Works turned out the last steam locomotive, *Evening Star*.

What was lacking for the railways, then as now, was any real analysis of what they were there to do. The unpublished Stedeford Committee was set up, numbering amongst its member a certain Dr Richard Beeching. Appointed Chairman of the newly formed British Railways Board, his masterwork was the report 'The Reshaping of British Railways' published in 1963. At the launching press conference he quoted Macbeth: 'If it were done when 'tis done, then 'twere well it were done quickly.' What he did *not* say is that Macbeth himself was referring to the coming assassination of King Duncan.

Much of the Beeching plan was concerned with ridding the railways of their economically hopeless elements. Politically, it caused a monumental furore. Basically, the plan dismissed local rural passenger services and stopping services on main lines, and criticised the excessive size of the freight and passenger rolling stock fleets. More positively, it looked forward to the quickest possible replacement of steam traction, and new markets for freight using modern containers on the new 'Freightliner' services. A later plan included proposals for the development of the major railway trunk routes and, by inference, the slimming down of the less major ones. Of particular import in 1966/67 was the completion of the electrification of the Euston–Birmingham–Manchester/Liverpool main line, though this was after Dr Beeching had departed.

Barbara Castle's Transport Act 1968, the same year as steam traction finally ceased, predictably had a different emphasis. The needs of the (eventually seven) major conurbations outside London were to be met by giving each of them its own Passenger Transport Executive, whose tasks included integrating bus and rail services in their areas and funding them as required. Outside those areas, specific Government grants were to be paid for socially necessary services, on a stabilised network. The Public Service Obligation approach was confirmed subsequently in European legislation.

This brought stability, albeit at a price. The modern railway developed in the 1970s, while service quality and provision generally surpassed anything which had been achieved previously. On the main lines it saw the introduction of the InterCity 125. Investment proceeded, albeit not as fast as many would have wished.

In 1979, the modern railway was still seen to be performing commercially less well than it might, especially in the face of the Conservative Government's wishes to contain their financial contributions. One outcome was the sector-led railway.

EXPRESS TRAIN & STEAMER SERVICES TO ISLE OF MAN

Left: Wholesale rebuilding of the West Coast main line, one of the 1955 Modernisation Plan schemes, took a decade to complete. Here, a Class 86/2 locomotive leaves the tunnels of central Birmingham behind as it gathers speed out of New Street with a London-bound express on 22 March 1980. *John Glover*

Above: The traditional railway had links with other, complementary, surface transport. At Bolton, this fine ship model was displayed on the up platform. The date is 14 June 1988. *John Glover*

Right: Minor branch lines had no place in the scheme of things; traffic levels were seen as too low to support specialised rail transport infrastructure. This Class 101 unit is at the Alston terminus of the branch from Haltwhistle, in October 1975, shortly before closure. *John Glover*

The present scene

Times change, but the railway system remains much in the form in which it was constructed. Railways are essentially long lasting; while technology advances and equipment is renewed, the physical railway itself remains more or less unchanged other than in a reduction in system mileage. The inevitable mistakes which are the lot of the pioneer are also with us. Of these, the most conspicuous is the result of the perhaps apocryphal story that George Stephenson used the biggest vehicle he could conceive to determine the loading gauge, to which virtually the entire system was built. This was a horse with a fully laden hay cart.

Today's railway faces a very different scene from that during most of its history. Railways have many strengths; for instance they:

● offer high speeds and/or high carrying capacity, with safety;
● are responsible for the movement of four-fifths of central London commuters, or about 800,000 people in each direction every day;
● have a modest land take in relation to line capacity; and
● can, if electrified, use coal, oil, nuclear or hydro-electric as indirect power sources.

But there are limitations also, and the business in which they do not excel is the economic movement of small volumes, whether they be freight or passenger. The exclusively provided railway infrastructure of track and signalling is costly, whether in terms of initial provision, its maintenance or its renewal. Rail is essentially a mass mover, preferably, though not essentially, over longer distances.

Also, railways cannot offer door-to-door transit for freight without transhipment, other than where industrial premises are directly connected by private siding. Passengers, also, have to get to and from stations; railways can never offer the door-to-door convenience of the private car.

Meanwhile, how has the railway been getting on in the postwar years?[4] A brief summary is shown in Table 2.1

Thus while the railway infrastructure, measured in terms of route miles, has almost halved, passenger traffic has declined much less significantly. Freight, though, has fallen dramatically. The railway has thus failed to maintain its carryings. This would be serious in a stable market, but the reality is that the market itself has expanded enormously. From being a prime market provider of both passenger and freight traffic in 1951, rail now accounts for a melancholy 7% of the UK passenger market and 9% of the freight.

There have, however, been many positive developments. From 1988, the non-commercial passenger railway was defined by the Government as excluding InterCity. The development of the InterCity shuttle concept was but one part of the response.

The efforts of Regional Railways deserve recognition. The introduction of Regional Express services linking (for instance) Liverpool with Ely on an hourly basis, with trains diverging thence to Stansted Airport and Norwich alternately, was a major and welcome innovation. Would any Franchising Authority dedicated to 'a regional or local identity' have thought up these economical services?

In the seven PTE areas, those authorities defined service provision requirements with some considerable precision, and accepted a collective bill of £115 million in return.

However, other Regional services were operated formally merely 'to provide a public service comparable generally with that provided on 1 April 1988'. In practice, there was little difference between that and the previous Direction, dating from 1975. The same Direction applied to NSE, and it was the Government who issued the Directive.

Times change, and the Regional Railways commitment to working in conjunction with local authorities to explore and then to maximise the benefits which rail could bring to their areas, especially in towns with 250,000-plus population, was a very positive move. This was a considerable

Right: **The new Woodhead Tunnel was completed in 1953, but this interwar electrification scheme was to have but a limited life. In December 1969, Class 76 No 26040 gets a Wath–Mottram freight on the move and approaches Penistone station.** *John Glover*

Table 2.1 BR rail traffic and infrastructure, 1951 to 1994/95						
Passenger miles	1951	20,793m	1994/95	17,806m	change	-14%
Freight net tonne miles	1951	23,268m	1994/95	8,073m	change	-65%
Route miles open	1951	19,357	1994	10,275	change	-47%

Above: Customer care was backed up with care for the staff and their dependents, as these well looked after displays outside 'the Ladies' at Bridlington showed on 30 May 1981. *John Glover*

Above right: The lesser known Beeching Report, *The Development of the Major Trunk Routes,* was published in 1965. While the ostensible aim was to show where investment funds would be concentrated, the message was that overcapacity in railways between cities was rife. Most of the routes survive today; those which do not include the Great Central main line and the Waverley route.

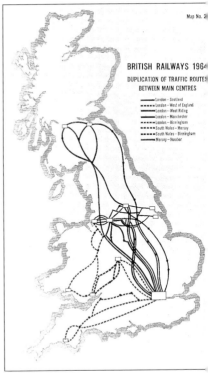

Map No. 2

BRITISH RAILWAYS 1964

DUPLICATION OF TRAFFIC ROUTES BETWEEN MAIN CENTRES

London – Scotland
London – West of England
London – West Riding
London – Manchester
London – Birmingham
South Wales – Mersey
South Wales – Birmingham
Mersey – Humber

advance over the 'do as you have always done' approach embodied in the PSO concept. On the other hand, where there is effectively no accountability, there is always extreme local reluctance to accept any lesser service levels, and politicians have always had the 1988 Direction to fall back on.

None of this is to decry the achievements of other sectors, though the change in what was once referred to almost disparagingly as 'Other Provincial Services' is remarkable. Yet, Regional Railways still only covered a small proportion of its costs through passenger revenues. Tight financial control is essential in the management of a service business; management must know what they are trying to do.

Something, as they say, had to be done. But what? We cannot, and must not try to, rebuild the past. The railway needs to move with the times, particularly in capitalising on the areas in which it can excel. At the same time it might be well advised to minimise its efforts on, and exposure to, the peripheral activities. Apart perhaps from London suburban services, it is nowadays far from a monopoly provider. Can the areas in which it is presently successful be extended?

Can the railway be successful in other areas too? What form of organisation and legal background is necessary to achieve change?

The seeds of what was to come were perhaps to be seen in EC Directive 91/440, which required the separation of railway accounts for service provision and for infrastructure. Separation of ownership, though, was not required. The intention was the opening up of access to newcomers and the establishment of a charging regime for infrastructure use. Importantly, this Directive applies only to international services between member states, which in Britain have had a low profile until the opening of the Channel Tunnel. The new arrangements were brought into force on 1 January 1993 (SI 3060/92).

Further developments, however, were to follow. Late in 1993, two proposals for EC Directives were published: one on the licensing of railway undertakings, and the other on the allocation of railway infrastructure capacity and the charging of infrastructure fees. The intention is that such matters would be uniform and non-discriminatory throughout the Community. These proposals became Council Directives 95/18 and 95/19 in 1995.

In Britain, the Government published the White Paper of 1992, which was followed by the Railways Act of 1993. A summary of the principal domestic primary legislation which has affected railways since 1947, and also that from Europe, appears as Appendix 1.

[1]*Government and the Railways in Nineteenth Century Britain.* H. W. Parris, Routledge and Kegan Paul, 1965.

[2]Parliamentary papers 1839, x, 132–3, quoted in Parris, op cit.

[3]*Modern Railway Operation.* David R. Lamb. 3rd edition, Pitman, 1941.

[4]Sources: British Transport Commission Financial and Statistical Accounts 1951, and British Railways Board Annual Report and Accounts 1994/95.

Left: Customer care is not a modern invention; at Thorpe Culvert on a frosty 22 January 1970, the conductor guard helps a passenger and her shopping off a Skegness–Firsby dmu. The platform has been largely cleared of snow. *John Glover*

The HST, IC125, call it what you will, was one of the most successful long distance trains to be produced in Britain. Before East Coast main line electrification, a down express regains the main line on leaving Peterborough in October 1981.
John Glover

Above: The check-in arrangements at Victoria for the Venice-Simplon Orient Express on 23 May 1985 did those involved little credit. The rail industry can do better than this. *John Glover*

Below: Passengers joining a Class 317 set forming the 1803 Liverpool Street to Cambridge as it arrives at Tottenham Hale on 27 April 1993. *John Glover*

The initial Government commitment towards change was announced by Her Majesty the Queen at the State Opening of Parliament on 6 May 1992:

'My Government are committed to increasing the role of the railways in meeting the country's transport needs. Legislation will be introduced to enable the private sector to operate rail services.'

First, the White Paper which preceded the Railways Bill, in which the Government's intentions were set out. Subtitled 'The Privatisation of British Rail', the White Paper was published on 14 July 1992. On objectives it was less than expansive, referring only to a wish 'to improve the quality of rail services'. The rest was method.

The White Paper

After an initial foray into the then British Rail of the 'not bad, but could do better' variety, the Government outlined what they saw as the six essential issues. These were:

- Safety — Standards must be maintained and bettered.
- Quality of service — All customers must be offered a higher standard of service.
- Essential passenger services — Continuing subsidy will be available to provide social and other benefits.
- Network benefits — The benefits of a single network for passengers include a national timetable and through ticketing.
- Employee opportunities — Enabled to transfer to the new companies and take a stake in private sector replacements.
- Environmental benefits — To continue to be developed.

Only six weeks earlier, the British Railways Board had completed their (re-)Organising for Quality initiative, which had been some years in the making. This created a number of free standing businesses, with both infrastructure and rolling stock assets as well as staff divided between them, leaving the Railways Board responsible for finance and to set policies and standards for the running of the railways as a whole. They were also there to settle disputes. Trading arrangements were set up to cover asset usage by other railway businesses. This was the end of the former regional railway organisations.

The operating businesses, managed through a total of 27 profit centres, were:

- InterCity
- Network SouthEast
- Regional Railways
- Trainload Freight
- Railfreight Distribution
- European Passenger Services
- Parcels

All this work came to naught; the preferred Government option was to dismantle the vertical integration of the railway where individual management teams were responsible for everything from infrastructure to operations — in short, all that they needed to provide the complete service to the customer. The Government decided to create a track authority (Railtrack), which would be separated from the train operating companies. The purpose of the latter was merely to operate passenger services until they were all franchised to the private sector. By then, Railfreight and Parcels would both have been privatised. 'This structure', said the White Paper, 'offers the greatest prospect for private sector involvement in operations...' However, it was made clear that the Bill would also provide for the eventual privatisation of Railtrack itself.

The Transport Committee

The House of Commons Select Committee on Transport, chaired by the late Robert Adley MP, reported in great detail in April 1993. This was *not* the Committee set up to debate the Bill. Their report ran to 172 pages, with the Appendices and Minutes of Proceedings accounting for a further 1,121 sides.

The report was critical of the Bill, and Adley was widely reported for his remark likening the effects of the then Bill to 'a poll tax on wheels'. A much abridged summary of the principal conclusions appears below:

- The Government is right to search for ways of improving rail services for passengers and freight customers.

- The test of any proposals must be their practicability, coupled with their ability to produce a sustained increase in investment.

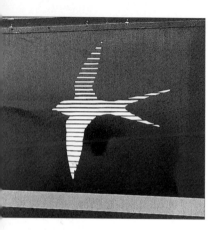

Above: The InterCity symbol as displayed on the side of an IC125. *John Glover*

- Investment is a basic prerequisite for success.

- The White Paper should have been preceded by a Green Paper discussing the role of railways, encompassed within an overall transport policy.

- Both for railway operating reasons and because of the implications for the viability of franchises, the scope for open access passenger services is very limited.

- Success in the franchising of passenger services needs:
  - a greater degree of vertical integration
  - greater incentives to Railtrack's efficiency
  - gearing the form and length of franchises to investment requirements
  - franchise areas chosen to preserve the coherence of the network
  - strict service standards and controls over fares to protect passengers against misuse of monopoly power; and
  - arrangements for continuing services in the event of an operator's default.

- The benefits to passengers of a national network must be preserved.

- The Government should commit itself to a system for co-ordinating coherent transport improvements across the country.

- An outline safety case should form an integral part of the formal franchise bidding process.

- A greater degree of simplicity could be achieved if Railtrack and the Franchising Authority were merged to form a single Rail Authority, though there would still be a need for an independent Regulator.

- In terms of international railway experience, the Government's proposals are novel and untested. The risk that something could go badly wrong is therefore higher than would otherwise be the case. This does not mean that the system cannot work, but considerable care and resources will be needed to ensure that it does work.

- Rail users will be the final judge on whether the legislation succeeds in maintaining the railways' social and economic obligations whilst creating opportunities for private profit.

The Railways Act

Meanwhile, the Bill continued its passage through Parliament, to become law as the Railways Act 1993 in November. It is a huge document, in three parts:

Part I deals with the provision of railway services;
Part II concerns itself with the reorganisation of the railways; and
Part III is the usual miscellaneous, general and supplemental provisions.

What does the Act actually set out to do? The following is an interpretation of the various Sections, starting with Part I. Many of those mentioned here briefly, such as the Franchising Director and the Regulator, we shall meet again in later chapters.

Introductory

The Act provides for the appointment and functions of a Rail Regulator and a Director of Passenger Rail Franchising (s1), the setting up of new rail users' consultative committees (RUCCs) for the railways (s2) and the Central Rail Users' Consultative Committee (s3).

Duties of the Secretary of State and the Regulator

The duties of each are to be exercised 'in the manner which he considers best calculated to:

(a) to protect the interest of users of rail services;
(b) to promote the use of the railway network in

Great Britain for the carriage of passengers and goods, and the development of that railway network, to the greatest extent that he considers economically practicable;

(c) to promote efficiency and economy on the part of persons providing railway services;

(d) to promote competition in the provision of railway services;

(e) to promote measures designed to facilitate the making by passengers of journeys which involve use of the services of more than one passenger service operator;

(f) to impose on the operators of railway services the minimum restrictions which are consistent with the performance of his functions under Part I;

(g) to enable persons providing railway services to plan the future of their businesses with a reasonable degree of assurance'.

Further duties refer to protecting the interests of users and also the price and quality of service offered by facility owners to operators. They also need to take into account the need for operational safety and environmental effects.

The Regulator has to take into account the guidance of the Secretary of State until the last day of 1996, but his need 'to have regard to the financial position of the Franchising Director' is perpetual (s4).

Duties of the Franchising Director

The Franchising Director has to carry out his task in a way calculated to fulfil the Secretary of State's objectives and instructions, in the provision of passenger services. He also needs to ensure that any payments made will achieve those objectives economically and efficiently (s5).

The outpayments by the Franchising Director are as a result of his entering into franchise agreements with passenger train operators. The franchise operator has the obligation to provide the services specified for the period of the franchise agreement.

Licensing of operators of railway assets

The Act establishes a licensing regime for the ownership and use of railway assets to provide passenger and goods services, and specifies how such licences may be modified. All operators of such assets must either hold a licence or be exempted. The Regulator may modify licences by agreement, or by making a reference to the Monopolies and Mergers Commission (s6–s16).

Access arrangements

It also provides that a railway facility owner shall, if so directed by the Regulator, enter into an access agreement with a train operator which allows the operator to use the owner's facilities on terms approved by the Regulator. The legislation on the highly complex question of access is spread across 12 pages of the Act (s17–s22).

Franchising of passenger services

The Franchising Director is placed under a duty to designate passenger services as eligible for provision under a franchise agreement (s23).

There are limited exceptions to franchising, in that railways as may be specified by the Secretary of State may be exempted (by the use of a Statutory Instrument). London Underground is the principal example and Heathrow Express is another, but others such as Tyne and Wear Metro and preserved railways would also otherwise need to be franchised. However, this Section would not prevent future Government changes of mind, such as exempting certain BR services from franchising (s24).

Public sector bodies may not be franchisees, apart from the Board under very restrictive circumstances (s25). Franchisees must be financially sound, competent and 'otherwise a suitable person' (s26).

Franchise assets will be transferred to the successful franchise bidder and returned at the end of the franchise period (s27). The franchise itself may include specification on fares to be charged and a mandatory requirement to participate in approved discount fares schemes. The Act specifies such schemes as those for the young, the elderly or the disabled (s28).

The next Section sets out the other terms and conditions of a franchise agreement, including the obligations of the franchisee to pay the Franchising Director or, alternatively, to be paid by him. It also contains the franchise term and its possibility of extension, rights of acquisition of property, and liabilities (s29). Provision is also made for the means of continuing a service once a franchise has come to an end and no further franchise agreement has been reached (s30). Franchise assets are not leases (s31).

Passenger Transport Authorities and Executives

The respective roles of the PTAs and the PTEs in connection with the franchising of passenger train services in their areas are also defined. Among them, the PTE has the power to specify the services to be operated, the service quality required and fares levels to be charged where it has an s20 agreement under the 1968 Act (s32–s36).

Closures

The Act establishes new railway closure procedures to replace those which applied previously to the British Railways Board. These have to take account of the now separate issues concerning the operation of services and the provision of the infrastructure, including depot facilities. The Franchising Director initiates the notifications of a proposed closure and the Regulator decides on its merits, attaching conditions such as replacement bus service provision as he thinks fit. The Secretary of State, however, only becomes involved if there is an appeal against the Regulator's decision. Lesser procedures are invoked where experimental new railway services are involved (those which have been running for less than five years) or the closure is classified as minor without service withdrawal from any passenger station and alternative routes are available (s37–s50).

Supplementary powers of the Franchising Director

The new legislation also provides for means by which the Franchising Director can ensure that services continue by subcontracting, for instance after a franchise comes to an end and there is no successor (s51), while he can also make agreements with the Board (s52). He may also form companies to undertake his own franchising or other duties — in a sense, to privatise himself (s53)!

This Section offers an interesting freedom to the Franchising Director in the way in which he exercises his franchising functions 'for the purpose of encouraging railway investment' (s54). This might be used to help address the problem of costly railway assets with long lives, such as new rolling stock, being unattractive propositions to a franchisee with a seven year contract.

Enforcement and winding up

The next Sections allow the Regulator and the Franchising Director to ensure compliance with the regulatory regime established by the Act and make provision in respect of railway administration orders, winding up and insolvency (s55–s65).

Consumer protection

Consumer protection and the relationship of the Regulator with other established bodies are clarified. The Regulator is given some of the functions of the Director General of Fair Trading under the Fair Trading Act 1973 and Competition Act 1980 (s66–s67).

Other functions

Other functions of the Regulator and the Franchising Director include the maintenance of registers, the collection of information and the publication of reports (s68–s75).

Consultative committees

The duties of the consultative committees are specified. These refer to the provision of railway passenger services or station services (s76–s79).

Information and interpretation

The Franchising Director can require information from licence holders or the Board and its subsidiaries, with penalties for non-compliance (s80).

Sections dealing with interpretation (s81-s83) include the definition of a railway as that of the Transport and Works Act 1992 s67(1), which is:

'A system of transport employing parallel rails which

(a) provide support and guidance for vehicles carried on flanged wheels, and
(b) form a track which is either of a gauge of at least 350mm or crosses a carriageway (whether or not on the same level), but does not include a tramway.'

So, now we know. It will be noted that this definition includes the Romney, Hythe and Dymchurch Railway on all three counts. The 15in gauge of the RH&DR equates to approximately 380mm.

Sometimes, the 1993 Act specifies that 'railway' shall have a wider meaning. This includes tramways, which are distinguished in the T&W Act 1992 by being 'laid mainly or wholly along a street or in any other place to which the public has access (including a place to which the public has access only on making a payment)'. They are also wholly or mainly for passenger traffic. In this wider context, 'railway' also includes other guided transport, other than trolleybuses or similar.

Part II of the Act (s84–s116) is concerned with the British Railways Board. The Act confers new powers on the Board with respect to the formation of subsidiary companies and the transfer by scheme of property, rights and liabilities in connection with franchising or in preparation for disposal to the private sector.

The Act also confers powers on the Secretary of State in connection with transfer schemes, including powers to give directions to the Board and to require information from it. The Secretary of State is also given the power to transfer to either himself or the Franchising Director the Board's function of making transfer schemes. The Act also makes financial provision relating to the Board as well as successor companies to the Board's undertakings.

Perhaps the most notable Section in Part II of the Railways Act is s113(1) which states: 'It shall be the principal objective of the Secretary of State ... to secure as soon as, in his opinion, is reasonably practicable the result that the function of providing railway services in Great Britain is performed by private operators.' This does, however, refer only to

Part II. In performing this task, s113 goes on to require the Secretary of State 'to have regard to the desirability of:

(a) encouraging competition between those who provide railway services;

(b) maintaining efficiency, economy and safety of operation in the provision of railway services in Great Britain;

(c) providing opportunities for persons employed in railway undertakings ... an interest in the ownership of the undertakings in which they are employed; and

(d) securing that the disposal takes place on the most favourable terms that can reasonably be obtained ...'

Readers will note that such a requirement would extend to any incoming government of a different political persuasion, to whom repeal would be the only remedy should they not wish to continue this policy.

Below: Joining the InterCity 1009 Birmingham International–Glasgow Central at Preston on 17 September 1993. *John Glover*

Part III is rightly referred to as Miscellaneous Provisions.

Safety, emergencies, security, etc

The Act makes provision with respect to the safety of the railways, which include control of the railways in time of hostilities or great national emergency. The latter even warrants a statutory definition: 'Any natural disaster or other emergency which, in the opinion of the Secretary of State, is or may be likely to give rise to such disruption of the means of transport that the population, or a substantial part of the population, of Great Britain is or may be likely to be deprived of essential goods or services.' Effectively, the Government retains the right to give directions to all those involved in service provision in such circumstances (s117–s121).

Statutory authority

If you are involved in running a railway, it is important that you are not open to a charge of causing a nuisance; this Section confers the status of statutory authority on operators and others (s122).

Miscellaneous

In a similar vein, the legal status of common carrier by railway, which obliges operators to refuse neither passengers nor consignments of goods is specifically removed, thus continuing a situation established under the 1962 Act (s123), while the Post Office can no longer compel railways to carry mailbags (s124).

The disposal of historical records or artefacts from the public sector is to be overseen by a new committee (s125).

Consequential changes in the powers and duties of the BRB (s126–s128) are followed by the power to make bylaws extend to new operators. These may be for matters as diverse as ticketing, smoking and obstruction of the railway (s129), followed by three pages of detail on the regulation of penalty fares by the Secretary of State (s130).

The Restrictive Trade Practices Act 1976 could make co-operation between operators over matters as varied as track access, ticketing or rolling stock maintenance extremely difficult. Such agreements may be exempted under this Section to ensure that network benefits are achieved and to avoid nonsenses similar to those which have occurred in the bus industry (s131).

The next Sections make provision in respect of the BT Police (s132–s133), pensions (s134) and staff travel (s135).

Financial provisions

The Regulations of the European Economic Community 1191/69 and 1893/91 for the payment of subsidy in respect of passenger rail services (the Public Service Obligation grant) themselves remain unchanged. The Railways Act designates competent authorities who may impose such obligations as the Secretary of State, the Franchising Director and, on a more limited basis, the PTEs and local authorities (s136).

The Act also makes provision for track access charges for freight operators to be paid for, in part or in total, by the Secretary of State, 'for the purpose of securing the provision of adequate services for the carriage of goods by railway'. There must be benefits of a social or environmental nature (s137).

Capital grants made under Section 56 of the 1968 Act have had an uncertain status if they were intended for use for access to airports or harbours. This new Section confirms that they may be thus used (s138).

The authority for freight facilities grants of the 1974 Act is re-enacted and made more general by applying a simpler public interest criterion (s139), while similar grants are available for freight by inland waterway (s140).

Financial assistance for the Board's management or staff buy-outs is available (s141), as it is for administrative expenses deriving from the Act (s142).

Supplemental

The remaining Sections are also administrative in nature (s143–154).

There are also 14 Schedules, which include amendments to existing Acts of Parliament and Repeals.

It is fully realised that the foregoing is somewhat indigestible, but it does represent a concise résumé of the Act's overall contents. It concentrates on some of the principal sections of the Act, though their individual importance is perhaps better judged with the benefit of hindsight!

Some aspects are conspicuous by their absence — for instance, there is no mention anywhere of Railtrack. Acts of Parliament provide powers and may also prescribe methods and introduce prohibitions. They may repeal earlier legislation. But they cannot undertake the job.

How this is being achieved is the subject of the succeeding chapters.

Railtrack

Railtrack is the organisation which owns the freehold and manages the track and other railway infrastructure. It is a commercial enterprise, earning a return from its assets. Railtrack is responsible for timetabling, train planning, signalling and control of the system, infrastructure maintenance and investment. It also co-ordinates the national passenger timetable.

The Government gave four main reasons for creating Railtrack:

- to provide a national infrastructure company which will give track access to every train operator on a fair basis;
- to secure appropriate levels of investment in rail infrastructure on a national strategic basis;
- to ensure that safety standards and procedures are co-ordinated in a clear and systematic way; and
- to ensure that timetabling is co-ordinated efficiently across the whole network.

Initially a Government-owned company, but privatised in 1996, Railtrack has an important role in the restructured industry. The company's objective is to provide the safe, efficiently-run network which is critical to the overall success of the railway.

'If it doesn't move, it belongs to Railtrack' is still a useful short description of the company's range of assets. Those assets consist of:

- 23,000 miles of track. In terms of miles of route, these are around 10,300.
- 90,000 bridge spans or culverts
- 40,000 property units. These include 2,500 operational and 1,500 non-operational stations, retail outlets on stations such as W. H. Smith, offices (eg those of catering companies), and the businesses occupying railway arches, comprising anything from a laser-gun shooting range to pine bed manufacturers.
- 1,200 signalboxes

The goals which Railtrack has set itself are:
- to provide our customers with safe, efficient,

Below: A typical Modernisation Plan reconstruction is Banbury. The 1040 from Marylebone formed of unit No 165026 is moving to the up line for the return journey on 8 April 1992.
John Glover

cost-effective services with targeted improvements in every activity;

- to develop a fair contracting relationship with our suppliers that builds in performance incentives;
- to offer our employees a fulfilling and challenging career in which all share equal opportunities; and
- to grow our business and increase the value to our shareholder.

Railtrack's annual revenue in 1994/95 was over £2 billion. The vast majority of this, £1,955m or 86%, was derived from selling track access to passenger franchise operators. Of the remainder, £191 million or 8% was from freight, £82 million or 4% from property rental and £47 million (2%) from open access passenger (as opposed to franchised) operators. These latter include all special trains and excursion workings, but also the operations of European Passenger Services Ltd.

It may be said that track access charges, which form a large part of Railtrack's income and TOC's expenditure are not a simple calculation. The structure of how charges were to be formulated was initially defined as follows, with proportions represented by each for a typical franchisee shown in brackets:

- Track access variable component (25%)

User-related charges refer to the costs incurred by an operator which vary with the volume of that operator's traffic, with the nature of the equipment used and, to some extent, with the timing of the trains concerned. This is further subdivided into track usage charges for 'wear and tear', and charges for electric traction current as might be applicable.

Peak charges are incurred where the railway is congested to the extent that there is an overall shortage of paths. A path allocated to an operator in the timetable is therefore charged to him, since it is not available to others. The charge is thus maintained, even if the path is not used.

- Track access fixed component (65%)

Directly-attributable fixed costs (30%). These long-run avoidable costs are specific to the services being provided by the franchisee, but do not vary with short-term changes in usage. Essentially, these are the parts of the railway infrastructure which would not be needed if the franchisee's services were not being operated. An example might be the bay platforms and the associated track and signalling used by local passenger services at a larger station.

Right: The clear sweep of the roof of Glasgow Queen Street (High Level) provides a pleasant airy atmosphere, although one could wish for a few more trains to fill the platforms (and hence pay access charges). No 37025 awaits departure with the 1645 to Dundee in June 1981. *John Glover*

Centre right: Cannon Street has undergone extensive reconstruction to accommodate Networker trains, but also to make the maximum use of the air space above it. The approaches were photographed on 27 March 1992. *John Glover*

Below right: Tame Bridge is a typical modern wayside station with minimal facilities. This one was built for CENTRO. Photographed on 8 April 1992 from the nearby road overbridge, it does demonstrate the long access routes which are necessary to provide for wheelchairs. *John Glover*

A complication arises if other franchisees share the use of that facility. If there are no others, then the whole of the costs could be saved, at least in the longer term. Where there are other operators, the avoidable elements are much less or even nil. Costs which are not attributable have to be treated as common costs.

Common costs (35%). There are three categories of costs as follows which cannot be allocated specifically to one operator and which would therefore not be avoidable if that operator ceased to provide services:

a) Those costs which can be allocated to specific sections of track but not to individual operators. Unless there is only one operator, these costs, such as the maintenance of a particular viaduct or tunnel, have to be divided between the operators using that section.

b) Those costs which can be allocated geographically. These are costs which are specific to an area but not to particular sections of track, such as those of a large power signalling centre.

c) Network costs, comprising essential overheads like administration and payroll costs, which can only be spread overall.

- Station rents (10%)

The vast majority of Railtrack's stations are leased to and managed by the passenger train operator who is the sole or perhaps main user of the station; this will normally be by a lease which is granted for

the same period as the duration of the service franchise.

Fourteen stations have been identified as being suitable for greater commercial trading and longer-term property development. Initially, these stations are operated by Railtrack itself.

Fig 4.1: Independently managed stations

Birmingham New Street	
Charing Cross	Euston
Edinburgh Waverley	Gatwick Airport
Glasgow Central	King's Cross
Leeds	Liverpool Street
London Bridge	
Manchester Piccadilly	Paddington
Victoria	Waterloo

Income from retail activity at stations is about £34 million per annum in total, of which this select list generates around £20 million. And what will this new approach mean? The following describes the Nagoya station development in Japan[1]:

The station will have a de luxe hotel, offices, a department store and shops, in a high-rise block both above and below ground level 'with an emphasis on the convenience, comfort and elegance that will characterise the sophisticated life-styles of the 21st century'.

It doesn't sound like any of the stations named above, does it? But, if the town centre moves away from the station, one remedy might be to develop the station in its own right to redress the balance. And, if the treatment described sounds slightly staid, why not a high-quality entertainment centre or theme park? We shall see.

Back to more mundane matters. The charging structure by Railtrack outlined above was intended to

give sufficient detail on how costs would be incurred by operating companies to help shape Railtrack's investment decisions. Track charges would reflect the quality of the track and other facilities provided during the period of the access contract. New investment costs by Railtrack would be recovered by variations to access charges as might be agreed between the parties concerned. These might, for instance, include the Franchising Director were he to specify service patterns which required infrastructure changes.

Fair enough, but what happens if the operating companies all disagree with each other as to what is

Below left: The fine South Eastern station at Rye; within there are two platforms and a passing loop on the otherwise 17-mile single track section between Appledore and Ore. *John Glover*

Below: A major reconstruction north of Croydon in the early 1980s saw a new flyover being built to carry the slow lines to and from Victoria over the up and down West Croydon local lines from Norwood Junction. *John Glover*

Right: King's Ferry lifting bridge dates from 1960. It provides the only connection between the mainland and the Isle of Sheppey. The bridge carries the Sittingbourne–Sheerness branch, singled at this point, as well as a road. Seen from the Swale station side on the mainland, a pair of Class 414 units return to the mainland on 25 March 1981. *John Glover*

Below right: The traditional level crossing gate, seen here at Lingwood, Norfolk, being reopened to road traffic after passage of a train. Perceptions of such arrangements as 'safe' are not necessarily accurate. As the author well remembers being told, if a train hits one of these gates, you have a large heavy missile flying through the air to keep clear of, as well as the train. *John Glover*

Hauled
Trains
Stop Here

needed and in what timescale? Who decides what is necessary and what is optional? How is technical compatibility between trains and infrastructure to be guaranteed? This extends to highly costly areas such as Automatic Train Protection (ATP) systems and the priority which may be attached to them.

Let us remind ourselves of a crucial railway characteristic. The need to have a specialised infrastructure, and to meet its provision costs, means in turn that it has to be well used. Heavy usage will help to spread Railtrack's costs sufficiently to keep unit charges down to an acceptable level for the operating businesses. The railway is volume hungry; the more traffic, the better. Line capacity is the most valuable resource, but its exploitation has to match the franchisee's (and any other user's) ability and willingness to pay.

Conversely, rail is at its least competitive where demand is low. After all, the track has still to be maintained and paid for. The Franchising Director needs to achieve value for money; this means maximising the benefits from paying support.

This is not to suggest that such railways are necessarily under threat. Service provision needs to develop to match changing social requirements, while economy of both operation and maintenance must be pursued.

The issue of how the cost of future rail infrastructure investment should be recovered through charges, important though it might be for small schemes, is of critical importance to Railtrack with really major investments such as those represented by the West Coast main line modernisation or Thameslink 2000 (both are examined later). These schemes have yet to be finalised, but it is for this reason that possible charging structures have been discussed here in some detail. Any scheme used should reflect the reality of the operating railway, be reasonably free of distorting effects over time and fair in its overall attribution of costs. But it also needs to be administratively practicable and allow Railtrack's operator customers to predict their future access commitments with some certainty.

However, access charges have also to be approved by the Rail Regulator, and the present situation will be found in that section.

So much for charges. On Railtrack's expenditure side, and apart from the 11,375 staff of Railtrack, most of whom are signalmen, there are the bought-in services of British Rail Infrastructure Services (BRIS), who presently undertake most of this work.

BRIS is divided into seven infrastructure maintenance units (IMUs), six track renewal units (TRUs) whose work area is self-explanatory, and seven design offices. The main areas of work covered by the IMUs are:
- track maintenance and inspection, covering up to two-thirds of IMU work;
- maintenance and inspection of signalling and pointwork;

Left: A standard automatic four-aspect colour light signal displaying a green aspect at Beckenham Hill on 21 March 1992. This is a test installation for driver only operation, with the camera providing a picture for the screen on the platform. *John Glover*

Above: An expansion joint in the track at Waterloo International. *John Glover*

- maintenance and inspection of power supplies and control equipment; and
- project work, especially for Railtrack's Major Projects Division.

Other work includes structure examination, maintenance and renewal, lineside work such as clearing vegetation and mending fences, dealing with adverse weather and the results of accidents, and safety management.

The railway of the future will see further changes. Track quality upgrading to meet greater tonnages and higher speeds on principal lines will make them more fit for their purpose, while simpler and cheaper methods of provision will have to be found for secondary routes. New track installation will have to be accompanied by less total track occupation, with the use of more technically advanced handling

Below: Flat junctions may cause capacity problems, but they do eliminate the need for costly flyovers. This is Weybridge from the west, with the Staines line diverging to the left of the picture. Given that there is a road overbridge at the far end of the platforms, readers are invited to ponder on the physical limitations of installing a grade-separated junction to the Staines line. *John Glover*

Bottom: A half-completed rationalisation scheme of what was once a standard double junction, pictured on 23 March 1992. This is Norton Junction, south of Worcester, where the line to Abbotswood and Gloucester (right) diverges from that to Evesham and Oxford (left). It was intended that these would become independent single lines from Worcester, thus allowing Norton Junction itself to be abolished. *John Glover*

equipment, while maintenance programmes will need to result in less frequent attention. There will need to be a detailed measurement of track condition and performance, with sophisticated programmes for giving it the necessary attention for maintenance and renewal.

The BRIS contracts with Railtrack are worth more than £1 billion a year. The BRIS units are themselves being sold; as existing maintenance contracts expire, new contracts will be let by competitive tender.

Railtrack's own organisation was divided into 10 geographically-based zones, which were later reduced to eight. The zones are the main interface between Railtrack's customers and suppliers, and with local authorities, local industries, user groups and others. They thus have a critical role in the long-term development of the network for increased use by both passenger and freight services. The zones, with their headquarters locations, are:

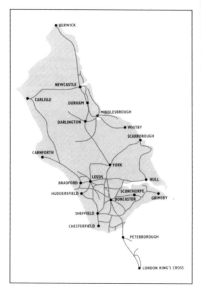

London North East (York). What might be termed the home territory runs south from Berwick-upon-Tweed to Newark and North Nottinghamshire, and thence via the East Coast main line to King's Cross. This latter includes the Hertford loop. Major conurbations include the Passenger Transport Executive areas of Tyne and Wear, West Yorkshire and South Yorkshire, while the route of the Midland line from Chesterfield to Leeds and Carlisle approximates to the western boundary.

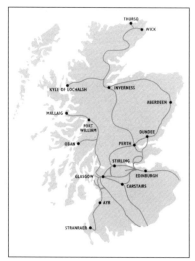

Scotland (Glasgow). Physically, this is the largest zone, on whose tracks run InterCity, rural and suburban passenger operations, and freight. Scotland has 11 train operating companies operating within the zone and has the largest suburban rail network outside London. These latter are run by ScotRail on behalf of the Strathclyde Passenger Transport Executive. A flagship service is the frequent Edinburgh–Glasgow Queen Street shuttle, for which ScotRail's plans envisage a 15min frequency in future. Beyond Inverness, the debate on how best to secure the Far North services rumbles on.

North West (Manchester). The North West Zone is bounded by Holyhead, Wrexham, Crewe, the Pennines and Carlisle. This encompasses a population of around seven million and includes the Greater Manchester and Merseyside Passenger Transport Executive areas. A full range of services is operated over North West Zone's tracks, including deep rural areas such as the Cumbrian Coast and the line to Blaenau Ffestiniog. Recent investment includes the IECC installation on Merseyside, while the modernisation of the WCML is likely to be a forthcoming task.

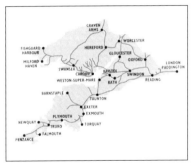

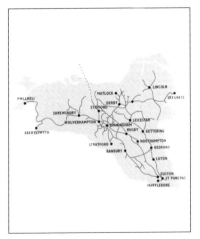

Midlands (Birmingham). The Midlands Zone links Skegness, via Matlock, to Pwllheli and south to the London termini of Euston, St Pancras and Marylebone. This includes the West Midlands Passenger Transport Executive area. Together with North West, Railtrack's Midlands Zone encompasses key parts of the national railway system, with the former London and North Western Railway main line as its core. But it also includes rural outposts such as the Leamington Spa–Stratford-upon-Avon branch, castigated by the 1983 Serpell Committee as having a (1981) revenue of a mere £76k, while direct costs alone amounted to £425k.

Great Western (Swindon). With the exception of the once-proud main line to Snow Hill and Birkenhead, this zone takes in nearly the whole of the former Great Western territory, plus all railways west of Exeter. Bristol and South Wales are the key industrial areas, while deep rural lines still abound, notably in Cornwall. The Great Western main line and its future electrification or otherwise will be a challenge for the zone, as will the developmental opportunities of Heathrow Airport rail links.

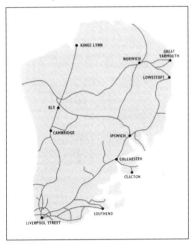

East Anglia (Liverpool Street). This zone comprises the lines of the former Great Eastern Railway and those of the Tilbury company. Both have heavy suburban traffics, while the GE also has InterCity and rural services. But Railtrack East Anglia also includes the North London Line, right through to its Richmond terminus. The North London is a multi-purpose railway, carrying north of London Eurostars, as well

RAILTRACK

as substantial freight from Thames-side and Felixstowe and an intensive local passenger service. What extra constraints will there be on the availability of train paths when the Channel Tunnel Rail Link starts to operate?

South West (Waterloo). The area is that of the former London and South Western Railway, whose Waterloo station is London's busiest, with 220,000 passengers daily. The Zone controls over 2,000 trains a day on behalf of 11 different passenger and freight operators. All major lines are electrified on the third rail.

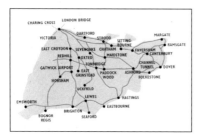

South (Waterloo). South Zone, smallest of all in terms of the geographical area covered, claims that its 1,800 miles is 'by far the most heavily used in the country, with nearly 220 million passenger vehicle miles travelled every year, more than any other zone'. The predominantly electric commuter traffic has also to cope with Eurostar and Channel Tunnel freight traffic, and Gatwick Express. The forthcoming Channel Tunnel Rail Link will require a substantial rethink of infrastructure requirements in conjunction with OPRAF and the TOCs.

Additional Railtrack headquarters directorates set standards and policy guidelines for the company. These include the Safety and Standards Directorate. Railtrack's Safety Plan provides strategic direction and sets objectives in terms of minimising accident rates. Other Directorates are Commercial, Engineering and Production, Finance, Government and Public Affairs, Human Resources, Legal/Secretariat, and Railtrack Property.

Of all the investment possibilities in the existing railway infrastructure, the West Coast main line modernisation programme is perhaps the most glamorous. However important they may be, overcoming the problems of the rising water table on Merseyrail's underground line, or IECC resignalling, come into the necessary but politically unexciting category. Total rebuilding of the WCML is another matter.

A full 30 years have now passed since main line electric trains began running accelerated schedules from Euston on 18 April 1966. By today's European standards, the schedules were pedestrian, but they were exciting enough then. 'For the first time in history, start-to-stop times at over 80mph appear in a British timetable. The 1700 from Manchester will be booked over the 65.1 miles from Rugby to Watford in 48min, at 81.4mph' enthused *Modern Railways*, noting that there would now be trains every two hours between Manchester and London, with extras in the morning and evening.

But, apart from extending electrification to Glasgow, not a lot has happened since. As Railtrack put it, 'Much of the infrastructure is now reaching the end of its life. It is becoming increasingly unreliable and the costs of keeping it going on a "patch and mend" basis are escalating'. The result was a study[2], in which the main aspirations of users were:
- reliability
- faster journey times
- increased line capacity
- increased options for freight, including a larger loading gauge.

The study team examined four business approaches to investment:
- the bedrock case, using the minimum patch and mend approach;
- the recovery case, using conventional technology to achieve a state of good repair;
- the cost-driven case, with major investment with the aim of cost reduction; and
- the market-driven case, with major investment designed to exploit market opportunities.

The task was to produce a single viable option, but this became a tiered solution consisting of:
- a core investment programme comprising the

Manchester and Liverpool are now 2 hours 40 minutes from London – city-centre to city-centre.
And from March 6th 1967, electrification to the Midlands will be completed.
London/Birmingham 1 hour 35 minutes.
London/Stoke-on-Trent 1 hour 58 minutes.

You can't beat us, so why not join us?

 Inter-City

Above: How the WCML business saw itself in 1966.
John Glover

optimum modernisation works that Railtrack alone can carry out; plus

● market-driven investment options for upgrading the line, presented as a series of options for discussion.

The core investment programme is designed to significantly improve safety, reliability and journey times, and to reduce costs. The enhanced upgrade options would permit significant journey time reductions for both passenger and freight.

The programme includes:

● the introduction of a cost-effective transmission-based train control system, replacing lineside signalling;
● Automatic Train Protection as an inherent capability of the train control system;
● the development of a single integrated control centre for the whole WCML;
● modernisation of other infrastructure elements, such as the improvement of power supplies to meet system performance standards; and
● an implementation programme involving minimum disruption to train services.

The core programme, costed at around £1 billion, represents the first stage of a modernisation programme that goes beyond bedrock and recovery. Incremental enhancements to the core programme, to meet further aspirations of customers and other users, are contained in a series of market-driven investment options, of which the key ones are:

● reduced journey times through a combination of track improvements (removed permanent speed restrictions, for example), the benefit of new technology (signalling, control and power), and the possibility of new rolling stock (such as tilting trains). These last, one might add, are not entirely new to the WCML.
● the potential for improved freight services including a wider structure gauge to incorporate piggyback and the possibility of longer freight trains.

The core programme meets many of the key aspirations, but the market-driven enhancements go further and bring attractive opportunities to operators and users.

The study demonstrated that benefits in terms of journey time reductions could be achieved, but that this required the co-operation of others, including decisions on the types of rolling stock used.

To justify such an investment, Railtrack needs to be confident that it would produce benefits in terms of long-term maintenance costs as well as passenger benefits such as greater reliability and journey time savings.

The market-driven investment options can be applied to some or all of the route sections of the WCML. However, the commercial viability of these investments depends on the desire of the future train operators to make use of them and negotiate track access charges to support their investment decisions to increase traffic (and therefore revenue) or reduce their train operating costs.

As part of the cost/benefit analysis, a socio-economic and environmental impact study was undertaken to examine in more detail the effects and likely benefits of the core programme and enhanced options on UK regions.

As to who benefits, these include the obvious ones of passenger and freight operators, but also those such as OPRAF, ORR, PTEs, the RUCCs, HSE, plus manufacturers and the infrastructure service providers. The study showed:

● InterCity would be able to provide faster, more comfortable, more reliable and more frequent services;

- InterCity would have greater flexibility in traffic management through improved train command and control systems;
- for Regional rail and North London services out of Euston, the remodelling of approaches to Euston together with the possibilities of double-decker commuter trains would increase reliability, improve services and increase demand while reducing costs;
- for services in the West Midlands, train control improvements would aid increased frequency of services in the Wolverhampton-Coventry corridor;
- longer freight trains and piggyback would offer greater opportunities to freight operators; and
- all trains would be afforded the improved safety benefit of the new train control system.

Without much service disruption during construction, passengers and business users would enjoy:

- a radically improved and more reliable service

Above: Tilting trains for the West Coast? Few ideas are really quite as novel as they might seem. APT 370003 and an unidentified trailing set arrive at Preston on one of the relatively small number of revenue-earning runs made before the cancellation of the project. *John Glover*

on the WCML;
- the ability to reach destinations punctually, faster and more often; and
- a competitive alternative to other modes of transport.

The new signalling technology would mean that existing systems could still be used while the new transmission-based system was installed, avoiding extensive service disruption during rebuilding.

Overall, the study concluded that:

- a core investment programme of modernisation works could be undertaken including a complete resignalling and comprehensive renewal of the

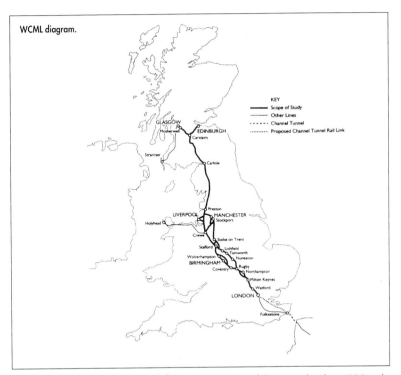

WCML diagram.

KEY
Scope of Study
Other Lines
Channel Tunnel
Proposed Channel Tunnel Rail Link

GLASGOW
Motherwell
EDINBURGH
Carstairs
Stranraer
Carlisle
Preston
LIVERPOOL
MANCHESTER
Stockport
Holyhead
Crewe
Stoke on Trent
Stafford
Lichfield
Tamworth
Wolverhampton
Nuneaton
BIRMINGHAM
Rugby
Coventry
Northampton
Milton Keynes
Watford
LONDON
Folkestone

track, electric power supply system and other infrastructure works;

• a series of options to further enhance or upgrade the line would offer, for example, improved clearances to allow piggyback freight operations and increase line speeds — potentially involving tilting passenger trains; and

• the core investment programme would also bring about a major improvement in safety through the provision of Automatic Train Protection (ATP), would improve reliability, lower ongoing costs of maintenance and operations, and radically improve a rail link which serves roughly a third of the UK population.

With such a prospectus, the premium for arriving at the right answer is equally high. However, the importance of InterCity is problematical, because although it accounts for 80% of Railtrack WCML revenues, InterCity represents only 16% of the trains using the line[3]. How, for instance, are the views and

aspirations of the Regional Railways TOCs to be taken into account? Such matters have to be resolved before real progress can be made.

Other major projects concern London, where a Director, London Projects has been appointed for Railtrack. A principal development is Thameslink 2000, which is an integration of rail infrastructure north and south of the Thames, with the key benefit of adding enough capacity to allow 24x12-car trains per hour (tph) to operate.

Costed at £650 million, this scheme requires less than a mile of new track. The main physical work in T2000 includes:

• Two new flyovers at New Cross Gate and Bermondsey to separate Network SouthCentral services.
• Extra platform and two new tracks at London Bridge.
• Additional track London Bridge to Borough Market (which involves demolishing two pubs).
• New Blackfriars station with entrances both north and south of the Thames.

- Closure of the 'Widened Lines' Farringdon to Moorgate section, since the extension of Farringdon's platforms to 12-cars can be achieved only at the eastern end.
- The severely congested King's Cross Thameslink station closed and replaced by a new station below St Pancras with entrance on Midland Road.
- Connection made to Great Northern, for which powers are sought in the CTRL Bill.
- Power supplies upgraded.
- Resignalling needed in central area.

This is Railtrack's first big enhancement project and it is essential to get the structure of the funding methodology for calculating track access charges right for the future.

Other major projects include east-west CrossRail between Reading and Shenfield, in whatever form it might eventually take, and Heathrow Airport rail links both to the north and south of the airport, with or without Terminal 5.

Potential conflict areas exist between such projects, whether for business reasons, geographical incompatibilities or diverse technical standards. What traffic volumes do we really envisage as attainable in the future, and what is the real ability of a given railway infrastructure to handle much higher traffic levels?

But schemes also need funding, and thus a promoter, if progress is to be made. The funding may be private, public or some combination, reflecting perhaps where the various benefits of the schemes are expected to lie. They also require one or more train operators.

It is in such difficult areas where future progress will perhaps be most eagerly awaited. Railtrack's Network Management Statement at the end of 1995 had perhaps rather less ambitious aims, but it did herald an investment programme for the next 10 years. This was a mixture of ensuring the infrastructure generally was in a satisfactory state of repair, but with special albeit unspecific attention being given as follows:

- For passenger traffic: attention to station access, interchange facilities between rail and road, information provision and service reliability.
- For freight: intermodal access to rail, loading gauge enhancement work and international traffic.
- For train operators: facilities which help them to reduce their operating costs, and to increase line capacity by eliminating bottlenecks where these are a constraint on service provision.

What might Railtrack seek to do in the Birmingham area, particularly at that notoriously difficult station of New Street? The station is presently being operated at well over its nominal capacity levels, with further growth expected. Signalling renewals are also needed. Shall we see a revival of the InterCity Heartlands proposal of 1992? This envisaged a new two-level station where the electrified Stechford — Aston — Bescot — Wolverhampton line, to be used by diverted Euston services, crosses above the NE/SW route. The Heartlands development area is seeking to generate 20,000 jobs and this project would help. The site is close to the M6 and station parking for 4,000 cars could be provided, while property gains would be achievable in the freed-up New Street.

On the other hand, InterCity would cease to run via New Street; trains on the NE/SW line might well save 10min running time by diversion, but all city centre passengers would have to transfer to or from local trains. A short stretch of new railway would have to be built, to allow Lichfield and Walsall line trains to serve the new station.

There are, of course, other possible solutions, but it will be interesting to see what transpires.

Finally, a view from the Regulator:[4]

'Railtrack has a central position in the railway industry. Thus not only is the future success of the railway in Great Britain dependent on Railtrack, but the success of Railtrack is dependent on those who provide services to Railtrack and on those who as train operators or funding bodies purchase services from Railtrack.'

[1] Annual Report and Accounts, Central Japan Railway Co, 1992.
[2] A Railway for the Twenty-First Century, The West Coast Main Line Modernisation Programme. Railtrack plc, February 1995.
[3] 'The Advent of Railtrack'. Robert Horton, Railtrack. Proceedings of the Chartered Institute of Transport, Vol 3, No 2, May 1994.
[4] Statement for Railtrack Prospectus. Office of the Rail Regulator, April 1996.

The new arrangements are nothing if not complex, and involve a large number of parties. Certainly, the wide network of contacts can be displayed differently, depending on which organisation is given centre stage. The version shown on page 48 and discussed further there is drawn to show the cash flows which result from matters as they were in the 1994/95 fiscal year.

The originator is the Treasury, which dispenses moneys via both the Franchising Director and the Passenger Transport Executives to the Train Operating Companies. The TOCs then have to pay the rolling stock leases, plus the track charges to Railtrack, as well as incurring the costs of running their businesses and collecting in the fares revenue.

Railtrack has to pay the infrastructure companies to maintain the system, but it also collects the access charges due from the freight operators as well as the passenger companies.

Finally, both BR and Railtrack have made sufficient profit to enable them to provide paper profits to reimburse the Department of Transport, which also makes an outpayment to European Passenger Services.

It will be evident that the situation will become rather more complicated with Railtrack as a private company and, as was concluded in autumn 1995, the rolling stock companies are sold off. It is not discussed further here, but in the view of the Select Committee on Transport, the annual subsidy requirement for the railway from the Government will rise by £700 million when the privatisation process is completed.

This chapter considers the Office of Passenger Rail Franchising (OPRAF), and the following chapter the Office of the Rail Regulator (ORR).

The Office of Passenger Rail Franchising

Let us go back to the origins of franchising. The basic principles were identified in 1859 by Chadwick, who argued in favour of competition *for* the market as opposed to competition *in* it. A competitive franchise confers exclusive but temporary monopoly rights on the franchisee in respect of specific operations.

Below: Peak arrivals at the main line inner-suburban platforms 1 and 2 at Waterloo on 6 September 1993. *John Glover*

The Government set out its stall on rail franchising during the passage of the Railways Bill. The following was contained in the Department of Transport's Consultation Document 'The Franchising of Rail Passenger Services', issued in October 1992:

- Central to the (Government's) proposals for passenger services is the intention to franchise their operation.' 'The Government wants franchising to be responsive to the market.' (Introduction, paras i and ii.)
- 'The aim will be to preserve as much flexibility as possible in ... the duration and geographical extent of franchises, and the functions to be carried out by franchisees'. There is a 'need to enhance competition ...' (para 3.1).
- The rights of a franchisee are 'to provide an identified group of services, be guaranteed the necessary track access to do so, receive passenger revenue and any other income his services generate, and, where necessary, receive subsidy' (para 4.1).
- The obligations of a franchisee are 'to provide at least the minimum level of service specified in his contract, and to meet at least the minimum standard specified therein, for the duration of the contract' (para 4.1).

These objectives have since been set out in formal instructions to the Franchising Director from the Secretary of State, and extracts from these may be found in Appendix 2.

OPRAF
Office of Passenger Rail Franchising

OPRAF's responsibility is to develop an attractive and saleable business opportunity, and also to sell the 25 passenger franchises. Although this is the remit, franchising is little to do with selling anything. A more explanatory way of looking at it is to think of the duties as:

'To receive competitive bids for a level of public funding to run a rail service for a period of time, the service levels themselves being specified to a greater or lesser extent.'

In letting the franchises, OPRAF need to ensure:
- service and value for the passengers;
- value for money for the taxpayer;
- success and profit for the franchisees; and
- long-term development of the railway.

There is a fundamental problem in balancing the aspects of service quality for the user, the constraints on taxpayer funding, and ensuring that the franchisee is not denied a successful business outcome. These tensions need to be present, but their resolution is a major challenge.

A threat to pursuing the objective of the long-term development of the railway is the need to accommodate immediate political objectives on funding. To what extent can (or should) the level of subsidy determine the quality of the railway which is offered? But what is a quality railway, anyway?

A suggested definition:
- driven by the market, rather than bureaucracy;
- responsive to customer needs;
- dynamic (well, we all want to be dynamic, don't we, but what does it really mean?);
- attracting capital from outside; and
- an industry where real improvements can happen.

There is a need to focus on commercial incentives.

Meanwhile, OPRAF is trying to improve quality, retain those network benefits which stem from a co-ordinated system, give the maximum autonomy to management, and control levels of risk.

Again, a political objective is to transfer risk from the public sector to the private sector. Initially, anyway, the competition is for the franchise, rather than head-to-head competition between operators on the railway itself. This is one of the reasons why a definition of quality targets is seen as so important.

What, then, does a franchise agreement offer? It gives the franchisee the right to run passenger services for a specified number of years, in return for an agreed level of public subsidy. It also confers ownership of the Train Operating Company running the franchise.

When it comes to bidding the next time round, this will be based on the deals which the potential franchisee can do, rather than having it all set up for them as with the initial round.

The characteristics of a franchise are:
- few fixed assets, such as a couple of photocopiers, and not much else;
- low initial capital requirements;
- the need to deposit performance bonds, to ensure that the franchisees do not lose interest in what they are doing;
- operational flexibility within the Passenger Service Requirement (qv); and
- a contractual entitlement to subsidy, offsetting fixed costs.

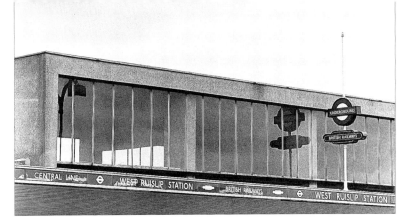

Above: The unified railways: British Railways and London Underground at West Ruislip. *John Glover*

Put another way, this last is a secure income which supports the businesses and also immunises the franchisee (and also the railway itself) from the year-to-year variability of public funding. The Treasury influence, in particular, is reduced.

The agreement between the franchisee and OPRAF has to get the balance right; whether between obligations and business freedom, or between risk and reward.

The Passenger Service Requirement (PSR) is the central element of the franchise agreement. It specifies the level of service which the franchisee *must* provide, on a route-by-route basis. Although he is free to provide more, he cannot provide less. The scheme is designed to prevent bidders from 'cherry picking'.

There are three types of passenger railway: essentially these are the InterCity, commuter and regional types. Some, such as Anglia, cover more than one type in different parts of their operations. The question which has to be asked is: what is OPRAF purchasing with taxpayers' money?

With InterCity services, previously provided more or less commercially by the British Railways Board, some attention needs to be given to frequencies. For commuter (and particularly London commuter) services, the peak demand has to be satisfied, but this gives the opportunity for off-peak services to be demand driven. For regional services, the service provision has to be justified and tightly specified.

The specification to safeguard passenger needs takes the following structure. The whole is remarkably complex and needs to specify:

- frequency
- times of first and last trains
- weekend services
- stations served
- journey time
- provision of through services
- preservation of key connections
- capacity standards, where applicable.

The key benefit for passengers is a new level of safeguards, under which for the first time the operator has clear obligations on a route-by-route basis, with every route and every station protected.

There is a long lead time when timetables are to be changed; this needs stringent controls in the PSR, including consultation. The benefits for franchisees are that their obligations are clear from the outset and that they have flexibility in how to respond to passenger needs.

A short extract from a specimen PSR is included as Appendix 3. However, it is difficult to avoid the conclusion that these are extremely prescriptive documents, with little indication of how 'the flexibility of private sector management will enable the railways to exploit fully all the opportunities open to them'.

Fares regulation is aimed at the control of monopoly power in areas in which it is thought to exist. The formula which has emerged where fares are to be regulated is the Retail Price Index +0% for three years from 1 January 1996, followed by RPI -1% for the following four years. What happens after that period is not clear.

This betrays an interesting political perspective rather than a railway one, in that previously ministers had been looking for real fares increases. The present formula, which relates to the seven-year

Above: Passengers besiege the 1109 Blackpool North–Manchester Airport at Preston on 17 September 1993. *John Glover*

franchise period, could conceivably even lead to fares decreases with very low inflation. This would play havoc with season ticket revenue; the London Tilbury & Southend is one business where huge amounts of money for annual season tickets are taken in fares revenue during December to avoid the January fares increases.

For commuter journeys, the pricing formula is to apply to standard singles and returns, and also season tickets, for journeys to work in and around the London area, Edinburgh and Cardiff. Some fares may rise by up to 2% above inflation but, if so, compensating changes below the regulated level must be made to other fares. In the Passenger Transport Executive areas, the PTEs themselves will regulate fares.

Elsewhere, Saver tickets are to be price regulated and, where there are no Savers, the unrestricted standard returns. Such tickets must:

- be valid for at least one month;
- be valid on any day of the week; and
- be valid at any time of the day, except that they need not be valid before 1030 (Mondays to Fridays) or for journeys leaving Greater London and other major stations near London between 1500 and 1900 (Mondays to Fridays).

The key point is that less onerous conditions may be applied by operators; what they cannot do is to be more restrictive. For instance, there is no *requirement* to restrict the use of the return portion of a Saver journey; only that operators may do so if they wish.

'OPRAF have sought,' it says here, 'to safeguard the essential features of the Saver ticket while leaving the operator some flexibility in the application of these restrictions.'

A second element is the quality of service performance. As the present Passenger Charter results show, results are patchy. From January 1997, in London, operators who fail to meet performance standards set by OPRAF will have their fares held down by up to 2% below the regulated level. If, on the other hand, they improve their performance, fares may be raised by up to 2% above the regulated level. Later, similar arrangements may be applied in Edinburgh and Cardiff.

The franchise process first required the creation of the 25 Train Operating Companies, each with its licence to operate and a safety case to demonstrate that it could manage operations safely and meet required safety standards. The subsequent stages are as follows:

- pre-qualification to bid
- issue of invitation to tender
- due diligence investigations
- bid made
- negotiation
- completion, including the formal acquisition of the TOC by the franchisee and final approval by the Rail Regulator.

Regrettably, the restrictions of the Financial Services Act 1986 inhibit open discussion; after all, these are businesses which change hands for only a nominal £1.

The transfer of the TOCs takes place with the necessary contracts in place relating to track, stations, depots, rolling stock and inter-operator agreements. Some of the bidders have clearly needed more time to come to terms with the magnitude of what they were proposing to undertake, and have betrayed a distinct lack of understanding of the rail industry.

Bid assessment needs to be based on the following criteria:

- value for public money
- financial stability of the franchisee
- risk transfer
- management competence
- employee involvement.

However, for the management of the franchise itself, this is essentially the beginning of a long-term relationship. The award to a bidder is only the start of a continuing arrangement, in contrast to the utility privatisations. Financial incentives are necessary to deliver improved performance; such incentives can be linked to matters such as punctuality and reliability — the essence of the customer charter objectives. Monitoring of customer satisfaction is also something to be imposed on franchisees. In any event, operators will need to produce their own customer charters.

It is the threat of competition, rather than competition itself, which could be destructive. It serves to concentrate minds. While breach and default of contracts can be pursued in the courts if absolutely necessary, OPRAF's preferred commercial approach is to prevent events which give rise to such costly and time-consuming actions from happening in the first place. This is much more productive than pursuing compensation issues to the bitter end. Few of those from the railway industry have any experience of procurement practices and contractual relationships, which is a weakness.

The principle of franchising is not without its detractors. There has been a long-standing antipathy to it in the Department of Transport. In March 1985, its Economics Directorate published a document 'Problems With Franchising'.

The context was the Government's proposal for the deregulation of local bus services. Many thought that bus services should instead be franchised out by the local authorities. The DoT paper concluded:

- Franchises afford a measure of protection to the incumbent, since the natural pressures are to accommodate operators' difficulties in order to maintain service and minimise public dispute.
- Franchises lead to substantial monopoly power, and its abuse.
- Franchises involve contracts between a public authority and a supplier, and require a performance specification. This can never reflect fully the detail of consumers' wishes. The specification must be imperfect, since the future is uncertain.
- The actual award criterion of the franchise will be to a degree artificial or obscure. It is impossible to reduce competitive bids to a single criterion.
- Franchisees may use any imprecision in the specification to their advantage. Only gross infringements can result in termination, since litigation and the exercise of penalty clauses is not costless.

Technically, local bus services are only partially akin to rail passenger services. Thus the capital requirements are of an entirely different magnitude, while the scale of rail operations is generally much larger. Rail services have to operate as part of a system, since the infrastructure of track and signalling is, at any one time, of finite capacity. As a business, the railway is characterised as having costly assets, which have an extremely long life.

Nevertheless, railway services are to be franchised. No doubt, events will as time progresses show either how successful franchising can be, or whether the DoT's concerns of a decade ago were justified. The Court of Appeal decision in favour of the 'Save Our Railways' pressure group that a PSR should provide for a continuation of pre-franchise service levels in order to fulfil a Government undertaking was perhaps an early skirmish. Though, as The Times pointed out in a leader, 'SOR suspicions that a minimum requirement would become a minimum service are ... hard to disprove'.[1]

[1]The Times, 16 December 1995.

Above: Milton Keynes Central, with a southbound InterCity West Coast train departing, shows its five-platformed layout. Platform 1 on the extreme left is a dead end, used for terminating trains from Euston only. Plenty of room for everybody — or is there? *John Glover*

Below: RES Class 47/7 No 47739 *Resourceful* heads empty stock from Bounds Green to Marylebone to form a charter service to Bicester. The train is seen arriving at Neasden Junction on 9 June 1995 for turning. The train is passing two Class 20s, Nos 20.118/69, hired to London Underground by RFS at Doncaster. *Brian Morrison*

The Rail Regulator

To ensure that 'fair play' is achieved, a Regulatory Authority has been set up. First, who are the users of rail services? For the Rail Regulator, there are two groups:
- The passengers of the train operating companies and the consignors using rail freight services; and
- Operators of passenger/freight/open access services, as users of Railtrack.

The Rail Regulator has three main roles:
- overseeing the arrangements for track access and charging over the whole network;
- promoting competition and preventing abuse of monopoly power and anti-competitive practices; and
- promoting the interests of consumers and ensuring that network benefits are maintained.

This is where the rail version of the nearest equivalent to the traditional Traffic Commissioner role in the bus industry is based. The Regulator sets out the rules and enforces them; he is also the arbiter. Attention is drawn to the scope for monopoly abuse in the railway; this is seen as being mostly in the London commuter network, and in the activities of Railtrack.

A further activity is the issuing of licences to railway operators. In general, all companies operating railway assets (a network, a station, a light maintenance depot or a train) need to be licensed. Licence exemptions will be granted to the operators of preserved railways and most other non-BR railways.

Licence holders are required to establish a policy to protect the environment from the effects of their activities. This includes compliance with environmental legislation, and using technological developments to upgrade their environmental performance.

Operators have to undergo a safety validation process overseen by the Health & Safety Executive before a licence is granted. The Regulator is responsible for enforcing licence conditions concerning such matters as policing, the environment, insurance requirements and through-ticketing.

On closures, the Regulator will make the decision on whether a closure should be allowed to occur, subject to reference of the matter by an aggrieved person to the Secretary of State. In exercising his functions with respect to closures, the Regulator will take evidence from the consultative committees, which it is also his duty to establish and maintain. The Regulator is able to attach conditions to any closures and enforce compliance with those conditions.

The Regulator has set out his stall on a number of issues. For the passenger railway (those pertaining to freight are discussed in Chapter 8), the principal ORR Policy Statements are as follows. These followed a series of consultation documents:

- Criteria for the Approval of Passenger Track Access Agreements (9/94)
- Railtrack's Track Access Charges for Franchised Passenger Services: Developing the Structure of Charges (11/94)
- Competition for Railway Passenger Services (12/94)
- Railtrack's Access Charges for Franchised Passenger Services: The Future Level of Charges (1/95)
- Ticket Retailing (4/95)
- Penalty Fares (for consultation, 10/95)
- Charter Train Services (for consultation, 12/95)
- Investment in the Enhancement of the Rail Network (3/96)

Each document is discussed in turn.

Criteria for the Approval of Passenger Track Access Agreements

As a general requirement, the Regulator will normally require to be satisfied that proposed access agreements are not framed in such a way that may unduly limit competition in service provision, create undue discrimination between users or represent abuse of a monopoly position.

A track access agreement is a bilateral agreement between Railtrack and a train operator. Areas of particular concern for the Regulator are likely to be as follows:

Timetable rights. These will need to be clearly defined and complete. They also need to be flexible enough to make changes, but not to constrain Railtrack in granting access rights to others.

Normally, the Regulator will expect the amount of track capacity taken up to be defined in terms such as the following:
- rights to run a number of trains in a given period, which might be a whole day or parts of the day such as the peak periods;

Performance incentives. Service performance can be adversely affected by infrastructure problems. In turn, these can result in reduced fares revenue and lower franchise payments. The Regulator will welcome arrangements which shift such income risk to Railtrack, provided they are workable! The Regulator may also require Railtrack to outline policy and procedures in respect of train service regulation. However, the net effect must work in the interests of rail users.

Charging arrangements and moderation of competition. Any exclusivity agreement will need to have alternative means of providing incentives contained in the franchise agreement.

Engineering strategy. The Regulator suggests that Railtrack and the operators may wish to negotiate procedures which compensate the operators for excessive line closures caused by engineering works and to reduce their payments if agreed renewals are not carried out.

Arrangements for operational disruption and contingency plans. Such plans need to exist, but the Regulator does not intend to review them in detail.

The Regulator holds the crucial key in approving access agreements. This duty will need to be exercised with great care.

- a right to run a train within a given broad time period (eg to run a train from Manchester to Bournemouth between 0830 and 0900);
- a right to run trains according to a specified interval pattern; or
- 'hardwired' rights to a specific time slot (eg the 'Flying Scotsman' must leave King's Cross at 1000. This is expected by the Regulator to be by exception only.

Operators and Railtrack may also enter into other contractual rights, such as times of first and last trains, connectional requirements, stopping patterns, through train requirements and use of rolling stock and train crew.

Specific matters of concern to the Regulator are likely to be:

- whether the proposed rights contain any in-built provisions which unduly reduce the capacity available on the network;
- the impact on the capacity available for other operators of any rights to service expansion; and
- the cumulative effects of restrictions on Railtrack's ability to flex an operator's timetable bid on the access rights which Railtrack can then agree with other operators.

Output standards. Operators will want to specify infrastructure standards to make sure that their business requirements such as ride quality and journey times are maintained, and that the access charges which they pay to Railtrack for the route will result in its being renewed as required.

Railtrack's Track Access Charges for Franchised Passenger Services: Developing the Structure of Charges

So, how are those access charges to be structured? The basis of the original unregulated track charges introduced in 1994 comprised:

- Track usage. These charges, 6% of the total, reflected the short-run 'wear and tear' effects on maintenance and renewal costs of running trains of different types for different distances.
- Traction current. This was the mechanism to recover the cost of electric current, varying geographically and by period of time, reflecting distance covered and type of vehicle. These accounted for 3% of charge totals.

• Fixed charge. This accounted for the remaining 91% and was payable irrespective of the number and types of train run, or passenger revenue.

From his consultations, the Regulator agreed that there was a need for operators to be able to determine how their actions affected the charges which would be levied, that some mechanism was needed to enable operators to make access cost savings if revenue fell and they wished to reduce services, while the whole structure needed to reflect greater variability in charging.

The Regulator's response was to require greater transparency through the disaggregation of Railtrack's charges. He also specified that operators should be able to seek from Railtrack an assessment of the effect of changes in both short- and long-term variable costs as a result of different access requirements. Any financial benefits which resulted, whether they concerned the reduction of costs incurred by Railtrack or the freeing up of more track capacity which another operator was prepared to purchase, should be shared between the original operator and Railtrack.

Competition for Railway Passenger Services

The main purpose is to try and reconcile the benefits to consumers which would result from open competition and the uncertainty among potential bidders for franchises that such competition would engender.

The Rail Regulator advanced two reasons for his concluding that it is necessary for competition between passenger train operators to be substantially restricted during the initial period. First, he recognised that the franchising process itself will produce increased competition because of geographical overlap, even without allowing for entry by so-called 'open access' operators. Second, the Rail Regulator noted that the railway industry is at an early stage in a period of fundamental restructuring and that unrestricted or uncontrolled competition would expose all parties to undue risks. These might negate the benefits of privatisation.

Consequently, no significant competitive new entry will be allowed before 31 March 1999 and substantial restrictions will remain for at least a further three years after that date. The restrictions will be reviewed in 2001, as will the level and structure of Railtrack's track access charges for franchised passenger services. The ORR has not determined the form which the competitive regime will take. However, the review will continue to reflect the policy

framework and it is likely that changes after 2002 will be incremental.

The Rail Regulator decided that it would not be appropriate to moderate competition by modifications to the current charging regime and therefore considered two broad options for implementing policy. One was on a case-by-case approach; the other was to use some kind of formula. The ORR decided to publish a framework, which would be used to establish the level of competitive new entry that would be allowed in each franchise area. Nevertheless, this would not preclude the investigation of individual cases.

The following detailed principles for moderating competition are to be adopted:

• Train operators should expect to face either early exposure to possible competition (as a result of the franchising process) or the firm prospect of increased exposure to competition during the term of their initial regulated access agreements.

• The potential financial impact of competition on franchisees should be limited and sufficiently predictable so that franchises are capable of being sold at a price the Franchising Director can afford.

• Franchisees should have the opportunity for commercial expansion as well as protection from excessive competitive risk.

• Entry of non-competing services should not be constrained.

• Within the controlled framework for the introduction of competition, the location of competitive entry should be market led rather than centrally determined.

• The new owners of the passenger railway industry should have some say over where they feel that protection from competition is needed, and decisions should, if possible, be taken in the light of actual experience of private sector behaviour.

Essentially, in the early years, involvement in operating passenger train services will be limited by the franchising process. Open access will be the exception, rather than the rule.

Briefly, the proposed mechanism consists of two stages. The first starts at the point at which the last of the BR TOCs has its long-term track access agreement approved and will expire on 31 March 1999, while the second stage will start at that point and expire on 31 March 2002. The protection is based on assessing the market in terms of point-to-point flows, reflecting the origin and destination stations of passengers carried by the operator.

In the first stage, operators will be able to

nominate a list of point-to-point flows, subject to limited constraints, on which new entry for scheduled passenger services will not be permitted without that operator's agreement. In advance of the second stage, operators will be able to nominate a revised list to be used as the basis for restrictions on nominated flows up to a threshold limit, which will be 20% of those flows by revenue. New entry will be unrestricted on any flows not so nominated. Finally, it should be noted that restrictions are subject to the access rights agreed between Railtrack and neighbouring operators which may well permit a level of inter-operator competition.

Railtrack's Access Charges for Franchised Passenger Services: The Future Level of Charges

The Regulator considered that Railtrack had scope to reduce its own costs by 3% a year and that the company could secure significant reductions in real terms in infrastructure maintenance costs. He also thought that access charges should cover depreciation on a current cost basis and that this should be enough to renew those assets, continue the

operation of the national network and the national timetable of services. To ensure that the network *is* maintained and renewed, the Regulator would monitor Railtrack's expenditure and performance at the national level.

Overall, and after allowing for inflation as measured by the RPI, the Regulator decided that Railtrack's charges should be reduced in 1995/96 for franchised passenger services by 8% and that they should fall by 2% per annum in real terms from 1996/97 onwards.

On property assets, the Regulator decided that variations in net income from property from the levels in Railtrack's projections should be shared between the company and train operators.

Access charges will be further reviewed in 2000, with the conclusions implemented from 1 April 2001.

Below: Specimen outward half portions of a Super Advance ticket issued on the Tribute system from Bath Spa to Loughborough in 1995. The journey is set out in detail, with some seat reservations. *Author's collection*

STD   SUPER ADVANCE   OUTWARD   VALID FROM   01 DECEMBER 1995
From BATH SPA   VALID UNTIL 01 DECEMBER 1995
To   LOUGHBOROUGH (LEICS)   Adult ONE   Child NIL
RouteAP BIRMINGHAM   VALID WITH YOUNG PERSONS RCD
Journey details (for codes see over)   Coach seat N/S Accom.
01DMR 11.28 BATH SPA   BRISTOL TEMPLE M 11.42 A 33F S SEAT
01DMR 12.04 BRISTOL TEMPLE M BIRMINGHAM N ST   13.40 B 01F S SEAT
01DMR 14.01 BIRMINGHAM N ST   NUNEATON   NRC   14.29 SUGGESTED SERVICE
                                               775
VALID ON DATE SHOWN BY SPECIFIED TRAIN   1 OF 2
Issued at   3271 33 15002057 16661 29NOV95 15.24 V-P C/CARD £19.45   For conditions see over

STD   SUPER ADVANCE   OUTWARD   VALID FROM   01 DECEMBER 1995
From BATH SPA   VALID UNTIL 01 DECEMBER 1995
To   LOUGHBOROUGH (LEICS)   Adult ONE   Child NIL
RouteAP BIRMINGHAM   VALID WITH YOUNG PERSONS RCD
Journey details (for codes see over)   Coach seat N/S Accom.
01DMR 14.39 NUNEATON   LOUGHBORO LEICS 15.17 SUGGESTED SERVICE
VALID ON DATE SHOWN BY SPECIFIED TRAIN   2 OF 2
Issued at   3271 33 15002057 16661 29NOV95 15.24 V-P C/CARD £19.45   For conditions see over

Ticket Retailing

In his consultation document, the Regulator said that he would be guided by the following issues:

- consumers should continue to enjoy widespread and easy access to through tickets;
- the new arrangements should assist in promoting the use of the network;
- within a framework which protects existing consumer benefits, operators should have scope to innovate and take advantage of the opportunities of new technology and new ways of selling;
- as a consequence of offering a greater range of choice to consumers, retailing is likely to become a more complex activity. The costs which operators may have to meet in order to satisfy the Regulator's requirements should be proportionate to the resulting benefits which consumers will enjoy; and
- to enable monitoring of compliance against the licence obligation, clear standards for levels of service will need to be established. So far as possible, these standards should be based on objective criteria.

In the light of the responses he received (and this included a debate in the House of Commons), the Regulator concluded that on the issue of ticketing, 'public opinion and public interest are at one'. BR's current arrangements (as at April 1995) for retailing tickets generally met customer requirements, and that to maintain them would not impose significant costs on operators for the immediate future. The approach of the Regulator would be that of incremental change, based on a clear definition of the service provided. This would cover:

- the product range of tickets sold at each outlet (based presently on APTIS and SPORTIS machines etc);
- the opening hours of ticket offices;
- more complex transactions, such as seat reservations;
- commission arrangements for selling tickets of other operators;
- how change might be progressed in the future, while avoiding undesirable side effects.

The arrangements will be reviewed in 1997.

Penalty Fares

Ticket sales income is worth around £2 billion a year to the railways; even a small percentage shortfall due to ticket fraud is therefore a sizeable sum in its own right. Penalty fares, in which a charge of twice the single fare may be made (minimum £10), is one way of combating the problem. However, as the Regulator has pointed out, Parliament was particularly concerned, when the original legislation was debated, that the innocent passenger should be given every protection from being improperly charged a fine, which is what a penalty fare amounts to. The Regulator is determined that high standards of passenger protection against being wrongly charged, should be maintained.

Consequently, he proposed that schemes should comply with the following:

- Passengers must be fully informed about what represents a valid ticket or permit to travel, before entering a penalty fares area or boarding a train subject to penalty fares, and what liability will be incurred by passengers who do not have one.
- For the liability to take effect, there must be a high degree of assurance of the passenger's ability to purchase first a valid ticket or permit to travel.
- Passengers must not be penalised if there was no adequate opportunity to purchase a valid ticket or permit to travel beforehand.

Charter Train Services

The charter market is very small but, according to the Regulator, it represents 'one of the few areas at present where third parties are seeking access to the network and promoting services'. There is thus some considerable determination on the Regulator's part to get the issue of costing and pricing right.

The document paints a picture of inexperience and uncertainty by TOCs, rather than deliberately trying to cause difficulties in the market. The Board are asked to produce a code of practice for its subsidiaries to set out how charges will be calculated and applied, as are the owners of RES.

The Regulator's proposed criteria are set out, which he will apply when considering access charges in contracts.

The Regulator's criteria are set out, which he will apply when considering access charges in contracts. However, the whole issue of charter services is to be kept under review and, if difficulties persist, the Regulator will seek further changes.

Investment in the Enhancement of the Rail Network

This document concentrates on new investment over and above the £3.5 billion required over six years for the replacement and renewal of existing assets. It depends, critically, on an effective partnership between Railtrack, train operators and funding bodies such as the Franchising Director, the PTEs and local authorities. In particular, a shared understanding of investment priorities and plans needs to be reached; Railtrack's annual Network Management Statement is seen by the Regulator as a means by which this can be developed.

The Regulator's general presumption is likely to be that ownership or operation of a railway facility should not be used to create a monopoly position for one or more train operators, and that capacity should be shared by all those able and willing to use it based on the public interest criteria in section 4 of the Act. Furthermore, capacity sharing must be on a fair financial basis, although vertical integration with the infrastructure owner having an interest in, or full ownership of, the operation of trains is not ruled out. However, the accounts of the infrastructure and operating arms would need to be fully separated as required in principle by European Council directives 91/440 and 95/19.

Railtrack is seen by the Regulator as having a vital role but, by having a monopoly position, train operators and their customers are dependent on the company. He therefore expects Railtrack to be proactive in the development of investment proposals, if they receive an appropriate return through access charges. These charges should be designed at least to cover avoidable costs, including that of capital. Generally, facility owners should receive a share of the benefits from investment, depending on the relative risks being taken by the parties involved and the source and level of the overall benefit. Exposure to revenue risks are particularly important here.

However, the charge structure might be designed to benefit Railtrack through higher returns if the company executes the project more quickly or more cheaply than originally expected.

New stations have been one of the most significant enhancement projects in recent years; in the seven metropolitan areas alone, 54 new stations funded by PTE capital grants have opened since 1988. Other schemes include line openings, electrification, resignalling and station refurbishment, with PTE infrastructure spend totalling £269 million over the period.

Finally, the Regulator points out that though licence and contractual provisions can offer a framework to help reach a shared understanding of investment plans, they are in themselves 'no substitute for effective co-operation between industry parties'.

Conclusions

Passengers want value for money, quality, reliability and an expectation of future investment in the railway. They also want energetic service development.

It is not the purpose of the Regulator to substitute his views for those of the competitive operator. However, he has to watch out for monopolistic practices. The Regulator must look to the needs of the users first. London customers are largely captive, while some InterCity routes have up to 40% of the market. There are better deals under the new legislation than the old. But, as Mr Swift, the Rail Regulator, told the House of Commons Transport Committee, 'If there are no benefits for consumers, the legislation was not worthwhile.'

Below: The 1034 New Brighton–Liverpool Central makes the Birkenhead North stop on 1 April 1995, formed of Merseyrail-liveried Class 508 No 508122. *Brian Morrison*

The three British Rail passenger businesses of InterCity, Network SouthEast and Regional Railways ceased to exist on 31 March 1994. The passenger railway was, instead, divided into 25 train operating units (TOUs). These were to become, after vesting, subsidiary BR train operation companies (TOCs). Each company operates under its own licence granted by the Rail Regulator, its own Railway Safety Case (approved by the Health & Safety Executive) and a track access agreement with Railtrack (approved by the Regulator). A wide range of station and depot access agreements (also approved by the Regulator), property leases and other contracts such as for rolling stock leases are also required by each train operating business.

While the operating companies mostly reflected their origins as being part of their former parents, some additional groupings were created. Thus, from Regional Railways South Wales and West, the Cardiff Valleys services were separated, and from Regional Railways North West we now have Merseyrail Electrics as a separate organisation. In the London area, NSE's Thames & Chiltern was subdivided into the Paddington group (Thames Trains) and the Marylebone group (Chiltern Railways). While Regional Railways Central continues as Central Trains, it no longer provides local services in East Anglia beyond Norwich, which have been transferred to the former Anglia Railways Train Services based on that part of InterCity. Another substantial change is in sleeper services, those to and from Scotland now being the responsibility of ScotRail.

However, the concept of geographically defined areas of operation is rather less relevant than it was previously. Since the infrastructure is now the responsibility of a completely separate company, Railtrack, the emphasis of the TOCs is on the services which they provide as businesses. The payments which they make, either to Railtrack in the form of access charges, or to rolling stock leasing companies (ROSCOs), are merely business outgoings — though this is not to suggest that they represent a minor part of their overall business expenditure. Somewhere in the order of two-thirds of their total costs appear to be in the right order of magnitude, although it will vary greatly. In theory, the situation is little different

Below: Aylesbury sees two-car unit No 165018 ready to leave with the 1815 to Marylebone as night falls on 3 October 1992. *John Glover*

from that applying to (say) the bus industry, where bus companies run vehicles (which they may lease, rather than own outright) on public roads provided and maintained by highways authorities and the Department of Transport (for which they pay excise duties).

Although most are still Board subsidiaries and hence subject to Board policies and guidelines, the TOCs now have a more direct responsibility for the specification and marketing of their services. In the railway before franchising formally takes place, the emphasis is on maintaining the *status quo*, though

stresses and strains are readily apparent in some areas. The débâcle over the future (or was it the lack of future?) of the London–Fort William sleeper service in late summer 1995 was a good example of how the concept of a public service obligation may conflict with hard commercial objectives. If the Franchising Director does not consider an InterCity service suitable for inclusion in his passenger service

Below: Figure 7.1, The circular cash flow in 1994/95, at 1994/95 prices.

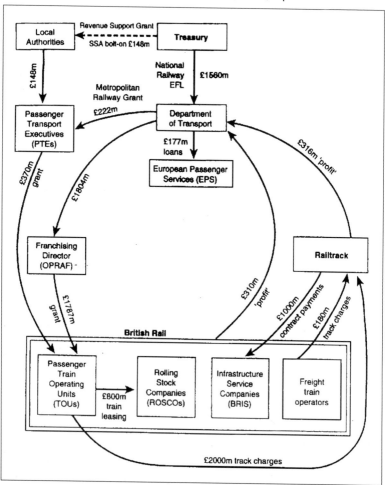

requirement (PSR), and the TOCs do not think they can run it profitably, what should happen and who is responsible for taking the decision? As an OPRAF manager opined subsequently, 'This just showed that these things can no longer be fudged.' This then leads to the PSR, considered in Chapter 5.

However, for the moment the OPRAF grant, which formerly came to the Board from the Department of Transport, effectively includes the Public Service Obligation requirement. The grant takes account of the need for additional outpayments to Railtrack and the ROSCOs as mentioned; the total OPRAF support grant paid in 1994/95 was £1748 million, or no less than 10.35p per supported passenger mile. At this level it represented a discouraging 79.8% of other passenger receipts. Similar changes have taken place in the value of the PTE s20 grants in their areas.

To summarise the new organisational arrangements, Figure 7.1 sets out the range of contracts and relationships as seen from the viewpoint of a Train Operating Company.

Let us now look at the overall passenger railway business itself and its characteristics. Firstly, on average journey length, distances on an average journey length, distances are relatively short. Over the whole BR network, this was 25.4 miles in 1994/95. However, when ordinary fares are separated from journeys made on season tickets, the average journey length associated with ordinary fares was 34.2 miles. This compared with seasons at 15.2 miles. In contrast, the average journey length on London Underground is 5.0 miles.

Secondly, season tickets must not be considered as a marginal element, since in 1994/95 they accounted for 47% or very nearly one half of all passenger journeys made on BR. Travel on ordinary fares (including all discounted fares) made up the remaining 53%. The revenues associated with ordinary tickets do, of course, reflect the longer average distances and are much higher than with seasons.

Above: The 0700 Edinburgh Waverley–King's Cross IC225 service passes Classes 31 and 56 on Peterborough depot on 2 June 1995, with Class 91 No 91006 providing power from the rear. *Brian Morrison*

The third point is that it would be fair to suggest that the railway as a whole encompasses a huge range of business types. For instance, Midland Main Line and Cardiff Valleys have little in common, be it in traffic volumes, service types, revenues or scale of operations. Generalisations are correspondingly dangerous!

However, on the basis of the foregoing, it is at least plausible to suggest that most passenger journeys are likely to be internal to one particular company's operation. Further, it is probable that relatively few journeys are made which involve the services of more than one operating company — unless that second company be London Underground. For the present purpose, London Underground involvement is not relevant, but it does perhaps indicate a way in which the London situation differs from that of the country as a whole, due to the sheer size of the capital and its surrounding residential areas.

In a 1970 exercise, the origins of East Coast main line passengers departing from King's Cross were identified. This was in the days when ticketing and revenue analysis were relatively primitive. To general managerial surprise, something like 40% of passenger journeys were found to originate somewhere on the (then) Southern Region. Today, many of those passengers might well be period Travelcard holders, but cross-London travel is perhaps likely to be the most common use of more than one train operating company's services.

Nevertheless, the situation everywhere does become more complicated, especially for the return parts of journeys, when more than one train operator provides services over a route.

Turning to the TOCs themselves, these are each considered in turn. The timetable referred to is that of 1995/96.

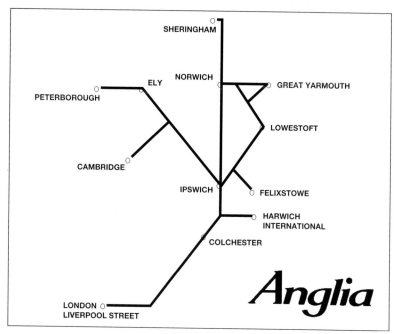

Anglia Railways Train Services Ltd

The core of Anglia's service is the old Great Eastern route from London Liverpool Street through Essex, Suffolk and Norfolk to the county city of Norwich. Electrification was completed in 1987, having previously been confined to the section southwards from Colchester.

Anglia provides the fast electric services under the InterCity banner between London Liverpool Street, Colchester, Ipswich, Stowmarket, Diss and Norwich; a few boat trains as required serve Harwich International (the former Parkeston Quay). Trains are made up of Class 86 electric locomotives, and mostly air-conditioned Mk2 rolling stock. Driving van trailers enable operation in a push-pull mode. Service frequency is basically hourly, increased to half-hourly at peak times.

Maintenance of all locomotives and rolling stock is carried out at Norwich Crown Point.

Away from the main route, Anglia provides local services between Ipswich and Lowestoft, Felixstowe, Cambridge and Peterborough; also between Norwich and Great Yarmouth, Lowestoft and Sheringham. All are provided by diesel units and frequencies are usually hourly or, in some cases, two hourly. In some instances, 'irregular' would be the only fair description.

Anglia's trains provide a modest 3.5 million train miles per annum, but an average passenger journey length of 59 miles (the London–Norwich distance is 115 miles) shows how much the business is dependent on the InterCity element of its carryings. This is reflected in the revenue per passenger journey of £6.67. A measure of train loadings is passenger miles per train mile, or the number of passengers on average on a train at any one time. At 86 for Anglia, this is close to the national average.

Operating performance in 1994/95 recorded reliability as 99.5% for the InterCity operation and 98.3% for local services. The standard in each case was 99.0%. For reliability, both recorded 90.7% against a standard of 90.0%.

In competitive terms, Anglia Railways have the Great Eastern Railway providing local services to Ipswich and Harwich and on all the Essex branches, while Central Trains reach Norwich from Peterborough in the west, on the route via Ely and Thetford. The provision of 12-car platforms on the fast lines at Stratford as part of the GE resignalling operation will also allow Anglia services to stop there as a matter of course.

Cardiff Railway Co Ltd

The Cardiff suburban and valleys services occupy but two platforms at Cardiff Central, the hub of the railway in the area and where connections are made with the InterCity services of Great Western trains and others. To the west of Central, the main route is south to Barry Island with a branch to Penarth, while the reinstated service via Fairwater to Radyr passes under the main line and then turns north.

Leaving Central to the east, the railway crosses the main lines to reach Cardiff Queen Street, in many ways a more satisfactory location for reaching central Cardiff. Train services then split to reach eventually no less than the five termini of Rhymney, Coryton, Merthyr Tydfil, Aberdare and Treherbert. Service levels are relatively intense, with half-hourly standard. This drops to hourly on the Fairwater–Radyr line, and north of Bargoed to

Rhymney. The Aberdare and Merthyr branches also have an hourly service. On the other hand, the combined service between Pontypridd and Cardiff Central runs every 15min, with three trains per hour to both Barry Island and Penarth.

Additionally, there are four trains per hour between Queen Street and Cardiff Bay (formerly Bute Road). Alternately, these start back from Caerphilly.

Maintenance of all the diesel units concerned is undertaken at Canton.

This is one of the smallest operations, covering as it does no more than 80 miles of network. Annual train miles are 1.8 million, with the average passenger journey length of 9 miles. This is reflected in the low revenue yield on a per journey basis of no more than £0.98. However, usage appears to be rather less than the timetable would suggest, with an average of only 29 passengers on a train at any one time.

Operating performance recorded reliability as 98.9% against a target of 99.0%. Reliability was recorded as 88.3% against a standard of 90.0%.

As with all busy suburban-type operations, Cardiff Railways make heavy use of the infrastructure provided. As an almost totally self-contained operation, neither the scope for competition nor the means of physically accommodating it is immediately apparent.

However, investment in new signalling and the infrastructure generally would be welcome, though this is at least as likely to take the form of service

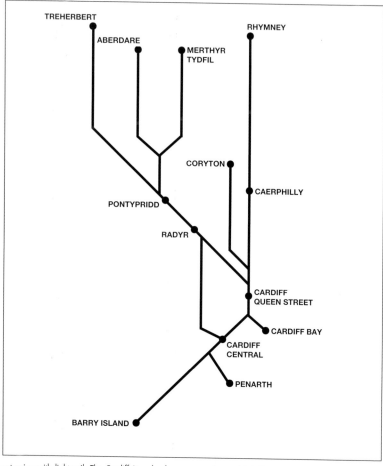

extension with light rail. The Cardiff Bay developers have long had a wish to see a new light rail system in the development area; the various possibilities for integrating it (or otherwise) into the Cardiff Valleys network are under discussion.

Central Trains Ltd

Central Trains is physically a large operation running from Birmingham to The Wash, and to central Wales as well. As such, it operates a diverse collection of services. These include the longer distance Express services of the mini-InterCity type, a range of more local services in country as diverse as the Welsh hills and the Lincolnshire fens, and an intensive suburban service for the West Midlands Passenger Transport Executive, aka CENTRO.

Alphaline services, provided by Class 158 Express units, operate between:

- Norwich, Peterborough, Nottingham, Sheffield, Manchester Oxford Road and Liverpool Lime Street (hourly)
- Cambridge, Peterborough, Leicester and Birmingham New Street (hourly)
- Birmingham New Street, Wolverhampton, Shrewsbury and Aberystwyth (alternate hours)

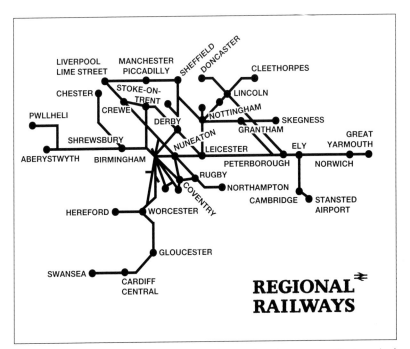

- Nottingham, Derby, Birmingham New Street, Gloucester and Cardiff Central (alternate hours)

Other longer distance services but on a less regular service interval include those between:

- Skegness, Grantham, Nottingham, Derby, Stoke-on-Trent and Crewe
- Grimsby Town, Newark Castle, Nottingham, Leicester and Coventry

Both these service types reflect the operational advantages of longer distance journeys. Rolling stock and train staff utilisation is improved, while commercially they may be very attractive. Even with shorter distance passenger journeys, a change of train may be avoided. (It may be noted that in these, as in other service descriptions, many intermediate station calls are omitted).

Central Trains operate rural services in Lincolnshire and in Nottinghamshire generally, including the Robin Hood line to Mansfield Woodhouse, the Ivanhoe line in Leicestershire and the Matlock branch in Derbyshire. North

of Birmingham, it operates to Chester and, of course, everything west of Shrewsbury, to Pwllheli and Aberystwyth. It also provides local services on the West Coast main line. Some services are of a seasonal nature, and this is now the only type of operation to take Central Trains to Great Yarmouth.

However, in the West Midlands conurbation CENTRO is a major customer, and railway services have been developed in recent years to the extent that there are now three cross-Birmingham lines. These are:

- Coventry, Birmingham International, Birmingham New Street, Smethwick Galton Bridge and Wolverhampton (half hourly)
- Lichfield Trent Valley, Sutton Coldfield, Birmingham New Street, Longbridge and Redditch (every 15 min within CENTRO area)
- Leamington Spa/Stratford-upon-Avon, Birmingham Snow Hill, Smethwick Galton Bridge, Kidderminster, Worcester Foregate Street and Hereford (mostly three or four trains per hour within CENTRO area).

Above: Smethwick Galton Bridge Low Level station sees No 323240 on the 1522 Wolverhampton to Coventry local working on 22 September 1995. The High Level station is above the Low Level and at right angles to it. *John Glover*

In addition, there are the other lines feeding into New Street, of which the only other local service is that from Hednesford/Walsall. The Lichfield–Redditch service was enhanced by electrification, while the 1995 opening of Galton Bridge brought about a new service pattern. While direct New Street services are denied for most of the time to those on the line to Kidderminster, the two-level interchange is the next best thing.

Maintenance of all the diesel units concerned is undertaken at Central Trains' Tyseley depot or Norwich Crown Point. Electric units are maintained at Bletchley.

As readers will have gathered, Central Trains is a large operation of 16 million train miles a year. The average fare paid is £2.31, for a journey of 23 miles average length. Train occupancy is 38 passenger miles per train mile, again relatively low. With all these figures, the diversity of the operation makes it difficult to draw worthwhile conclusions.

Reliability as measured for the Passenger Charter varied between 98.5% and 98.8% against a target of 99.0%; punctuality was 92.8% in East Midlands and Lincs, 87.5% for inter-urban services and 89.0% in Mid Wales and the Marches. All were against a target of 90.0%.

One of the operational problems of the area is Birmingham New Street which, since the growth of traffic due in part to CENTRO's activities, is regularly operating close to capacity. The re-establishment of Snow Hill, now once again a through station, goes at least one part of the way to freeing up New Street and allowing a new station to be constructed for the International Convention Centre on the ac lines north of the city centre.

The Ivanhoe and Robin Hood lines both have more work to be completed on them, as has the Walsall–Rugeley link. Throughout the area, new stations are being proposed.

Light rail schemes will be introduced in the West Midlands and perhaps in Nottingham, though their effect on rail services is unlikely to be more than marginal.

Competitively, Central Trains runs parallel to other operators in a number of areas, most notably on the WCML in the Midlands. The interaction with InterCity West Coast in the Coventry-Wolverhampton corridor is a long-standing problem related to capacity as well as the fares policies of CENTRO. In the south east of their operation lies Stansted Airport, presently with but a token service. Will airport expansion bring opportunities for Central Trains, or is the link from Stansted Airport to Cambridge and beyond a lost cause?

◣ *Chiltern Railways*

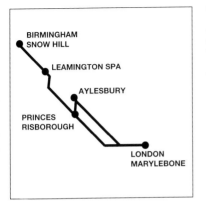

BIRMINGHAM
SNOW HILL

LEAMINGTON SPA

AYLESBURY

PRINCES
RISBOROUGH

LONDON
MARYLEBONE

Chiltern Railways Co Ltd

The Chiltern lines saw the first of the 'total quality' approaches, under which investment moneys were concentrated on the line to effect a steep change in the quality of service offered. Related and major works included the provision of new trains, new signalling and upgraded stations. A healthy growth of patronage ensued. There are but two lines, with a connection between them. The whole is the result of agreements and co-operation between the Great Central, the Great Western and the Metropolitan Railways in the 19th century.

Services over the Aylesbury branch from Marylebone consist of a basic twice-hourly stopping service to Aylesbury via Amersham, with a journey time of about 56min for the 37.75 miles. These services, of course, have the Metropolitan Line services of London Underground running in parallel and then sharing the same tracks between Harrow-on-the-Hill and Amersham.

On the High Wycombe line, services from Marylebone run alternately to:

- Aylesbury via Princes Risborough;
- Birmingham Snow Hill via Princes Risborough and Banbury; and
- intermediate stations to High Wycombe.

It might be noted that the journey for the 43.25 miles to Aylesbury, reached this way with a limited stop service, takes only about 4min longer than via Amersham. The Chiltern lines could indeed compete with CrossRail.

All services are provided by the Class 165 'Turbo' units of mixed 2-car and 3-car varieties. Maintenance is undertaken at Aylesbury.

3.3 million train miles are operated in the course of a year, with the average passenger journey length of 24 miles. This reflects the outer suburban nature of the operation, with services nearer London often provided by London Underground's Metropolitan or Central Lines. Average revenue per passenger journey is £3.24, and there is an average of 49 passengers on a train at any one time.

Operating performance recorded reliability as 99.2% against a 99.0% target. Punctuality was 93.6% against a standard of 92.0%.

This is another of those largely self-contained railways, though the Midlands as a destination may offer further possibilities. However, some uncertainty attaches to CrossRail which, if built as previously intended, would result in the end of the Chiltern line service to Aylesbury in its present form.

Cross Country Trains Ltd

Cross Country Trains is essentially the non-London InterCity business, built around what were once the locomotive-hauled North East-South West services such as Newcastle-Bristol, plus later additions like Manchester-Poole. Essentially, all were (and are) centred on that linchpin of the railway network, Birmingham New Street, while few services venture near London.

Today, Cross Country services originate on both the East Coast and West Coast main lines, sometimes from as far north as Aberdeen or Glasgow. South of Birmingham their destinations include Swansea, Penzance, Poole and Brighton, as well as Paddington and, surprisingly, Ramsgate! This last, culled from the diagram in the BR Annual Report 1994/95, appeared to justify its inclusion by being the 1995 destination of one train on a summer Saturday service from Birmingham New Street and return, operating on only six occasions between 22 July and 26 August.

Service provision resembles a four-pronged web, with services lessening in frequency as distances from Birmingham increase. Starting from New Street, the main thrust is to Newcastle, with about half the total service operating via Wakefield Westgate and Leeds rather than via Doncaster. North of Newcastle, the service is in the residual category, since Edinburgh trains mostly reach Birmingham via Preston.

The WCML operation, from Glasgow and Aberdeen as well as Edinburgh, divides to run a couple of services via Manchester, but most continue

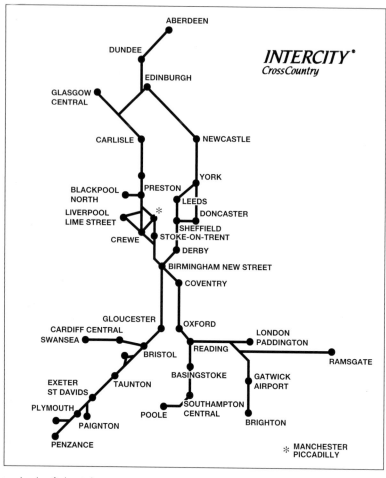

INTERCITY
CrossCountry

* MANCHESTER PICCADILLY

on the electrified main line via Warrington. Some services originate from Liverpool Lime Street, and rather more from Manchester Piccadilly.

To the south of Birmingham in the south-easterly direction, apart from a couple of trains which terminate at Birmingham International, all reach Reading. Rather more than half the services reverse, to continue to Bournemouth or Poole, while the rest continue to Paddington apart from a couple for Brighton. On the line to the south west, a third terminates at Bristol Temple Meads and most of the remainder at Plymouth, though a few workings reach Penzance. Paignton is another destination reached,

and so is Swansea, but both for a single daily train only.

The total number of trains per day is around 16 from Birmingham New Street on all the corridors, apart from a rather heavier service south from Manchester Piccadilly.

As always with an operation where the infrastructure used is only electrified in part, and not even all on the same system at that, the choice is between locomotive-hauled stock and time-consuming traction changes, and diesel operation throughout. The need for *en route* reversal, or otherwise, is another factor. Cross Country operate a fleet of InterCity 125 trains plus Class 47 diesels and Class 86 electrics for the hauled stock.

Further Cross Country services are those to Manchester Airport, from Edinburgh. These, operated by Class 158 Sprinter Express units, run via Carlisle. One train from Edinburgh divides at Preston, with a portion continuing to Liverpool Lime Street.

The fleet operates about 9.5 million train miles a year, from that measure making Cross Country about an average size Train Operating Company. However, as might be expected from a business which includes the longest continuous runs on BR such as the 704 miles between Penzance and Dundee, the average passenger journey length is a healthy 103 miles. Trains also have a reasonably high occupancy rate of 119 passengers on average, while the revenue per passenger is £9.27. While this is less than for the top earning companies, Cross Country has virtually no opportunity to tap the London business market, albeit that it is well placed to benefit from Birmingham traffic. The consequential lack of first class traffic depresses earnings, and the company's IC125 fleet have only one first class trailer car per set. The main business is long distance leisure travel, plus some modest commuting flows.

Sleeper operation has now ceased.

InterCity Cross Country provide IC125 services to Waterloo for Eurostar purposes, though, unlike those of Great Western, these trains are hired to European Passenger Services Ltd and are not available for use other than by bona fide Eurostar passengers. There is one train in each direction on Mondays to Saturdays between Waterloo and Manchester Piccadilly and between Waterloo and Edinburgh.

Operating performance for reliability was recorded as 99.5%, better than the 99.0 target, but punctuality at 82.6% (90.0% target) put the company at number 52 out of the 53 routes in the league. Cross Country does of course have to interwork with many other passenger companies; there is also freight and, as the Department of Transport has delicately observed, 'there are many individual freight flows on the InterCity Cross Country routes'. Whatever the reason, punctuality in 1994/95 clearly left a lot to be desired.

As to the future, Cross Country operates over a wide range of routes. Together, these allow plenty of development scope, with the possible additions of other destinations such as those made available during the summer period only. On the other hand most routes are at least in part covered by the services of other operators; inter-availability of tickets is likely to be an important requirement.

The rolling stock is not among the more recent acquisitions, and the replacement requirement will have to be tackled in the not too distant future.

Gatwick Express Ltd

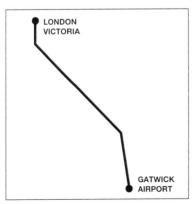

The former Gatwick Racecourse station on the Brighton line, built in 1891 but rarely used since the outbreak of World War 2, was rebuilt, resignalled and renamed Gatwick Airport on 28 May 1958. Very soon afterwards, aircraft started to use the airport itself, built, so it was reported at the time, 'to relieve London Airport of Channel Islands air traffic and later, probably, of some cross-Channel services'.

Well, much has changed since those days, when the service provision from Victoria was a two-car unit detached every half hour from the back of a Bognor Regis train. Traffic growth produced first the economical 4VEG stock variations of the 4VEP trains with luggage racks substituted for some seats, but the overcrowding of the Network SouthCentral commuter services was becoming unbearable. The economical solution adopted was to convert some surplus air-conditioned Mk2f stock for use as trailers and with internal layout changes, match them with a 2HAP driving motor car with its seats removed, plus a Class 73 — and there was Gatwick Express!

Gatwick Express services run between London Victoria and Gatwick Airport only; there are no

Left: The so-called Class 423/1 4VEG units were 4VEP conversions, with some second class seats removed in the saloons and luggage racks substituted. This is unit No 7906 at Haywards Heath on 3 October 1979. *John Glover*

intermediate stops and no service variations. Departures on a daily basis (how many TOCs advertise the same timetable every day of the week?) are every 15min from Victoria from 0530 until 2000. Outside these times the frequency reduces to 30min, with a 5hr shut down at night. Journey time is 30min for the 27 miles.

In the reliability stakes, 98.8% of services operated (target 99.0%), with punctuality recorded at 87.8% against a 90.0% target.

The Gatwick Express fleet consists of 13 Class 73/2 locomotives, 74 coaches made up into two- or three-car trailer sets of Class 488, and 10 Class 489 GLVs. All are based at Stewarts Lane. Even the coaching stock is nearly 25 years old, while the locomotives are nearer 30 and the GLVs older still.

This is a modestly sized operation, with its annual 1.2 million train miles the lowest of any TOC, barring only the Isle of Wight. Nevertheless, Gatwick Express average revenue scores at a remarkable £7.50 per passenger journey, given the fixed journey length. This works out at no less than 28.7p per passenger mile. Train loadings equate to a very average 78 passengers.

Competitively, Gatwick Express has to contend with Network SouthCentral, whose four fast trains per hour calling intermediately at Clapham Junction and East Croydon take 33min, or 36min with a Redhill stop as well. This is very little different to the 30min that Gatwick Express offers. Additionally, Thameslink provides four direct services per hour from London Bridge in 30 mins, or a little longer from Blackfriars or City Thameslink. So, there are alternatives. It will be interesting to see what transpires; positive specific branding and the possibility of offering check-in deals are clearly on Gatwick Express's side. But what arrangements might be worked out on the ticketing side, especially in conjunction with the airlines?

Great Eastern Railway Ltd

Shorn of its Cambridge interests and indeed those beyond Ipswich, the Great Eastern Railway of today is not the same as the pre-Grouping company. This is real commuter railway territory, albeit that it shades off into the lesser used parts of the system towards Sudbury or Harwich. Something like three-quarters of the company's income is derived from season ticket (or Travelcard) holders; the maximum single journey distance which can be travelled is a fraction over 70 miles.

There is substantial peak supplementation, but the analysis which follows is confined to the inter-peak period. Even interval services here are the order of the day, and they dovetail neatly together. The service pattern of trains originating from Liverpool Street, in summary, is like this:

- All stations to Gidea Park — 3tph
- Stratford, Ilford, Romford and all stations to Southend Victoria — 2tph
- Stratford, Ilford, Romford and all stations to Southminster — 1tph
- Fast to Billericay and then all stations to Southend Victoria — 1tph

The Southend/Southminster trains fit together neatly to give as nearly as possible a regular 20min service on the Southend branch.

- Chelmsford, Colchester, Manningtree and Ipswich — 1tph
- Shenfield, Chelmsford, Witham, Marks Tey, Colchester, Wivenhoe, Thorpe-le-Soken and Clacton — 1tph

The Ipswich train connects into a 1tph Colchester, Colchester Town and all stations to Thorpe-le-Soken

Right: First of the Class 315 emus to sport Network livery was No 315812, ready to form the 0633 departure from Liverpool Street to Gidea Park on 21 June 1986. *John Glover*

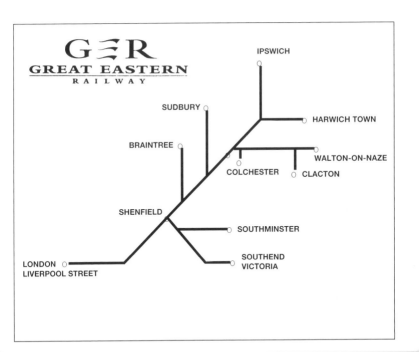

GƐR
GREAT EASTERN
R A I L W A Y

IPSWICH

SUDBURY

HARWICH TOWN

BRAINTREE

WALTON-ON-NAZE

COLCHESTER   CLACTON

SHENFIELD

SOUTHMINSTER

LONDON
LIVERPOOL STREET

SOUTHEND
VICTORIA

Gidea Park

315 812

service, which itself then has cross-platform interchange at Thorpe with the Clacton train, before proceeding to Walton-on-Naze itself. The Ipswich train also connects at Manningtree with a 1tph Ipswich, Manningtree (reverse), and all stations to Harwich Town service. There is also a connection at Marks Tey from the Clacton train into the Sudbury branch 1tph shuttle and at Colchester into the 1tph Anglia service to Norwich. Finally, there are:

- Romford, Shenfield, all stations to
  Colchester Town   1tph
- Romford, Shenfield, Chelmsford, Witham and
  stations to Braintree   1tph
- between Romford, Emerson Park and Upminster
  only   2tph

The Great Eastern example is given in some detail, to show what can be achieved within a reasonably uncomplicated network and where only two operators are involved.

In performance terms, reliability at 99.3% is in excess of the 99.0% target, and punctuality at 91.3% comfortably bettered the 88.0% charter aim.

Inner suburban services are provided by the fleet of Class 315 units dating from 1980, while the outer services are the preserve of Class 321s (1989) and Class 312 (1978). All are based at Ilford.

Train miles at 6.2 million per annum are not huge, but the railway is very well used at 138 passenger miles per train mile. Revenue per passenger journey is £2.42, with average journey length at 19 miles.

The GE resignalling by Railtrack is slowly reaching fruition, having been under way since 1985. When complete, this will allow many further revisions to services.

Of perhaps greater import is the possibility of major investment schemes in the area. These are the Channel Tunnel Rail Link, for which an underground box would be constructed north of the present Stratford station and which will contain both an international and a domestic CTRL station. Then, for the GE services themselves, the CrossRail link in tunnel to Liverpool Street, Farringdon, Tottenham Court Road, Bond Street and Paddington, thence on to the GWML, still has a place in the in-tray. A Shenfield–Reading service would form part of the total proposed service, but how would this fit into the franchising regime…?

In the 'definite' category is the forthcoming Jubilee Line opening to Stratford, while access to Docklands is likely to increase in importance.

Below: Great Western trains offer only a limited service to Great Malvern. One of these is the 1020 from Paddington, the 'Cotswold and Malvern Express' seen here arriving on 23 March 1992. John Glover

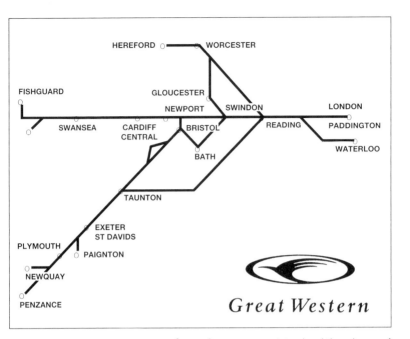

Great Western

Great Western Trains Co Ltd

The name 'Great Western' is indelibly associated with I. K. Brunel, its illustrious engineer. Today's Great Western company provides InterCity services from its Paddington terminus westwards to Reading, and thence by a number of routes, to destinations in a wide arc from Worcester and Hereford in the north to Penzance in the south. The entire operation is in the hands of IC125 units.

One of the difficulties of operation on this route is the nature of the territory it serves. With the exception of South Wales and perhaps Bristol, there is a lack of large centres for which to aim. With the Bristol Channel neatly dividing up its territory, Great Western has little choice but to run separate services over several routes. As a result, service frequency on each is perhaps less than could be justified were some combination of services possible. In turn, this makes future investment options such as electrification difficult to justify, due to the large number of track miles involved relative to traffic potential.

The principal services by Great Western are those running hourly from Paddington to Bristol Parkway, Cardiff Central and Swansea, and to Bath and Bristol Temple Meads. Most hours, there is also a departure

for Taunton, Exeter St Davids and Plymouth, many of which are extended to Penzance.

Other services are more of the occasional nature; thus, there are four trains per day to Gloucester and Cheltenham, one of which continues to Worcester Shrub Hill. But Worcester also sees three Great Western trains which run from Paddington via Oxford and the Cotswold line. These all continue to Great Malvern and two of them on to Hereford.

Another occasional projection of London trains from Bristol Temple Meads is to Plymouth, perhaps diverting via Weston-super-Mare. Fishguard Harbour receives minimal service, in connection with Rosslare boats only. Other destinations served, such as Newquay, Paignton and Pembroke Dock, are restricted to the summer months or summer weekends.

A recent introduction, in connection with Eurostar services from Waterloo to Paris and Brussels is a single IC125 working from Cardiff to Waterloo and vice versa. For similar reasons, the 'Night Riviera' sleeping car service between London and Plymouth/Penzance also now runs to and from Waterloo.

How does the service perform? Reliability was recorded as 99.3% for 1994/95 (target 99.0%); punctuality was 90.9% against a 90.0% standard.

Half of Great Western's business is leisure related, with business travel accounting for a further third. This company, too, is in the middle rank when it comes to annual train miles, recorded as 7.3 million. Average passenger journey length is 81 miles, roughly equivalent to a journey from London to Swindon. For this journey length, the average fare paid is £10.79. At 52, the average train occupancy is also close to the BR mean of 46.

To the south of the Great Western main line lies Heathrow Airport, which is to be linked by the Heathrow Express Railway for non-stop trains to Paddington. With at least a chance that Terminal 5 will be constructed and Heathrow air traffic grow further, what role might there be for the railway in providing surface access? The Great Western could indeed be an important player in this game, provided that line capacity is not too serious a problem.

There is not a need in itself to divert the main line trains through the airport, with all the extended journey times which this would entail, but it could be one of the possibilities. This would make electrification of the GWML a necessity, since diesel traction will not be permitted on the airport's railway. Apart from any other factor, there will be no suitable ventilation ducts.

Meanwhile, County Councils in the West Country and South Wales would like to see the Great Western upgraded. They recognise that the IC125 fleet will soon be reaching its quarter century and that electrification schemes (everybody's favourite?) take time to plan and implement, even if the finance is available. But deciding which of the rail routes could justify electrification, and whether it should be to their ultimate termini or stopping short (and, if so, where?), is another matter. To which, one might add, 'don't forget Birmingham'.

InterCity East Coast Ltd

Although not the 'Premier Line' in the historical sense, the East Coast main line has nevertheless built up an enviable reputation for quality and speed over the years. The long-delayed electrification of the principal trunk routes was eventually completed in 1991. This encompassed Glasgow Central via Carstairs, Edinburgh and Leeds (and now Bradford Forster Square), but did not extend to destinations such as Harrogate, Hull, Teesside or Aberdeen. The result is that IC125 sets still make an occasional

Below: A Mk4 set, with a Driving Brake Van leading, passes the Ferme Park flyover a little to the north of Harringay, on 15 May 1993. The train is the 1105 Leeds to King's Cross. *John Glover*

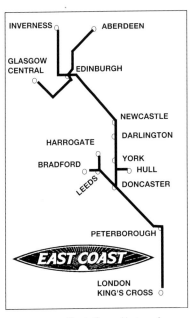

Reliability was precisely on target at 99.0% for 1994/95; punctuality was rather less satisfactory at 87.6%, against a 90.0% standard.

At 9.3 million train miles a year, service provision is similar in volume to that of Cross Country. Average journey length is 161 miles, the highest of any TOC and about the distance from London to Doncaster. Encouragingly, the revenue per journey is also a system high at £18.73 and so is train occupancy at 190 passenger miles per train mile.

The East Coast route does not enjoy quite the same number of commercial centres as does the West Coast, but both business traffic and tourism (notably to York, Durham and Edinburgh) are valuable earners. North of Doncaster additional services are operated by Cross Country, while trans-Pennine services join at York. On the northern part of the route there is thus some scope for competition, while the Midland main line has always operated some service to Leeds via Sheffield — if only to reach their stabling point at Neville Hill. Still, two can play at that game; the 'Master Cutler' once reached Sheffield via Retford, while at Grantham there is a route to Nottingham... Neither, though, is electrified, and in all cases competition might have to be based more on price than on speed.

InterCity West Coast Ltd

The first main line terminus in London was Euston, opened in 1837 as the terminus of the London and Birmingham Railway. The original station would not be recognisable today, after the massive 1960s style rebuilding undertaken as part of the electrification of much of the network radiating from it.

Yet, the priority given to the West Coast main line in the massive investment programme outlined in the 1955 Modernisation Plan was surely right. This is a main line railway whose owners were not much interested in suburban traffic; there was more profitable business to pursue. Indeed, commuting has never reached the epic proportions enjoyed (if that is the right word) to the south and east of London.

Today, Euston's major traffics are with the West Midlands and the North. The hourly midday service pattern offers the following, principal calling places only mentioned:

- xx00   Manchester Piccadilly, via Stoke-on-Trent
- xx10   Liverpool Lime Street, via Stafford
- xx15   Birmingham New Street, via Coventry and Birmingham International
- xx40   Preston, via Crewe; alternate trains extended to Glasgow Central

appearance at King's Cross. Most services are provided by the Class 91 locomotives, Mk4 coaching stock and Driving Brake Vans, which together make up the 31 IC225 electric sets. All trains are fully reversible, so that remarshalling is not needed at any point.

The hourly interval pattern from London during the day usually consists of one Glasgow Central via Edinburgh train, one to Leeds and one to Newcastle, but up to six trains may leave King's Cross in the busiest hour. Other intermediate terminating points used are York and Edinburgh. Aberdeen has three through trains from King's Cross in the course of a day, Bradford Forster Square has two, while Hull and Inverness each have just one. Harrogate has one train via Leeds, but in the up direction only.

With stops at York and Newcastle only, the 1500 Mondays to Fridays from King's Cross arrives at Edinburgh at 1905 (fastest time in the public timetable). This equates to an average 96mph capital-to-capital speed. This however is with a maximum 125mph speed; the 225 km/h (or 140mph) capability of these trains has yet to be exploited.

Maintenance and servicing for InterCity East Coast is carried out at Bounds Green, Neville Hill, Heaton and Craigentinny.

● xx45   Wolverhampton, via Coventry,
Birmingham International and New Street

During the business peaks, some additional trains
are run, but supplementation is kept to a minimum.
Additional services are those to Holyhead in
connection with boat sailings.

The principal rolling stock consists of a mixture of
Class 86/87/90 locomotives and coaching stock of
the Mk2 and Mk3 air-conditioned varieties.

Despite a perceived bad performance, reliability
was recorded at an acceptable 99.4% for 1994/95
(target 99.0%), while punctuality at 89.5% just failed

to match the 90.0% standard.

InterCity West Coast trains cover 11.0 million
train miles a year. The other indicators show a
similar pattern to InterCity East Coast, in which the
average passenger journey on InterCity West Coast
is 140 miles, with an average fare paid of £16.62.
Train occupancy rates are slightly lower too, at an
average of 165.

As with the East Coast, it is the northern part of
the line, in this case beyond Birmingham, where the
presence of Cross Country trains is felt. However, on
the WCML there are also outer suburban services
parallel to the InterCity West Coast services to

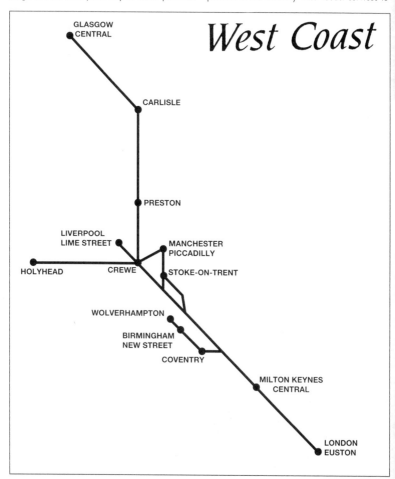

West Coast

Above: Class 87/0 No 87020 *North Briton* hurries through South Kenton on 27 January 1994 with the 1100 Euston–Manchester Piccadilly. *Brian Morrison*

Birmingham. London to Birmingham itself, which includes Snow Hill, is of course possible by a number of routes, all of which are beginning to offer different fares. Further north there are also other operators whose services can or do impinge on InterCity West Coast; be it not forgotten that the Scottish sleeper traffic now brings ScotRail to Euston.

The most important future project is the resignalling and effective rebuilding of much of the infrastructure. There are a few small matters, though, to first be decided:

- What exactly, in technical terms, should be done?
- Who will promote it?
- What timescale is achievable?
- How will the capital costs be paid for?
- What constraints or opportunities will the package place on the route's operators?
- What benefits will it bring, and for whom?

To resolve those problems satisfactorily, for this and for other major projects, will perhaps represent one of the greatest tests of the efficacy of the post-1993 Act railway. What, one might ask, has the answer to such problems to do with letting competitive seven year operating franchises?

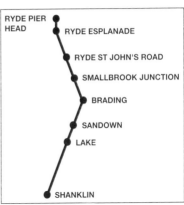

- RYDE PIER HEAD
- RYDE ESPLANADE
- RYDE ST JOHN'S ROAD
- SMALLBROOK JUNCTION
- BRADING
- SANDOWN
- LAKE
- SHANKLIN

Island Line Ltd

The Isle of Wight network at its peak stretched to 55 route miles. As one commentator has observed, 'With the wonderful benefit of hindsight, it now appears that much of the railway expansion on the Island was carried out with the heart, rather than the balance sheet as the main *raison d'être*.' Closures started in 1952, and by 1966 the only railway left (apart from what is now the preserved steam line) was the 8m 31ch between Ryde Pier Head and Shanklin.

This line survives today, electrified and with its second generation of electric rolling stock, albeit that

Class 483 cars of unit No 007 head a formation of two sets arriving at Ryde Pier Head on 17 June 1992. *John Glover*

the latter is well over half a century old. Formerly owned by London Underground, the ex-1938 tube stock trains hardly look as though they are in their element as they battle up the 700yd of Ryde Pier in a stiff breeze. A force eight and water coming over the tracks on the pier is enough to stop them. This is a very limited operation; even the newly extended Bluebell Railway in Sussex has a greater route mileage, while some its rolling stock is actually newer!

Services operate twice an hour over the length of the (now) mostly single track line. Indeed, in the six miles south of Smallbrook Junction, the only switch and crossing work is that for the passing loop at Sandown, where there are also a couple of sidings for permanent way purposes. In itself, this is a limitation on the maximum service which can be run. Just for the record, the fastest end-to-end journey time of 21min equates to an average speed of 24mph, including stops. The 2-car Class 483 trains (as they are known to officialdom) are limited to a maximum speed of 45mph anyway.

Island Line remains a vertically integrated or unified railway, in the sense that the infrastructure has not been split off from operations to a separate company. Its small size and isolation from the rest of the network has perhaps been the main reason for the Island Line being treated differently from the remainder. The TOC is the infrastructure controller. Railtrack own the infrastructure, but Island Line lease it from them and have close liaison with the South West Infrastructure Maintenance Unit which has a permanent way team on the island.

Likewise, Ryde Works, where maintenance work is undertaken, remains part of Island Line. The works is largely self-contained; only wheel turning and major work on the traction motors has to be sent away to the mainland. Not that the operation is very large; train miles are about 200,000 per year and the whole is run by 46 staff. Remarkably, both the average passenger journey length of five miles and the average fare paid of £1.00 are very similar to London Underground. A dispiriting average train load of 16 passengers is the lowest of any TOC, by some margin.

In performance terms, service reliability was 99.2% for 1994/95 (target 98.5%) and punctuality was 96.2% against a target of 93.0%. One of the problems of Island rail operation is the desirability of meeting Wightlink's catamaran from Portsmouth at Pier Head. If the catamaran is delayed, there is little point in the train departing, but it can play havoc with the rest of the timetable.

But there is another way for 'classic' — ie non car-bound passengers — to cross from Portsmouth to Ryde, and this is by hovercraft from Southsea Hoverport to Ryde Esplanade. This service is operated by Hovertravel.

Given also that minibuses are now allowed on Ryde pier, the future of Island Line looks less secure than perhaps it once did. The Isle of Wight enjoys relatively comprehensive bus service provision; it is much to be hoped that the railway can offer a worthwhile contribution to the travel needs of the island in the 21st century.

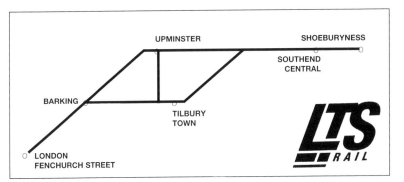

LTS Rail Ltd

The Tilbury has always led a largely self-contained existence, even given its acquisition by the Midland Railway in 1912. Although freight usage to and from places like Dagenham, Purfleet and Thames Haven requires access to the rest of the network via Barking and Forest Gate, the passenger services rarely stray outside the local area.

This is real commuter territory, with the Fenchurch Street terminus receiving nearly 30,000 arrivals in the morning peak. This is more than the combined totals of Euston, Marylebone and Paddington, and has to be absorbed by a four-platformed station consisting of two islands, with a (nowadays) twin-track approach.

Off-peak, though, it is a different story, with little more than 3,000 arriving. Fenchurch Street is a fine destination for city workers, and with a walk to Bank LUL station can be used for access to the West End,

but it is hardly ideally sited for the off-peak shopping or leisure traffic.

Service provision is correspondingly peaked; it is the off-peak basic timetable which is described here. This consists of six trains per hour from Fenchurch Street, two of which run via Tilbury and terminate at Leigh-on-Sea. The other four, two of which omit Limehouse, West Horndon and Laindon, run main line through to Shoeburyness. An additional and connecting hourly service runs to Upminster, Ockendon, Chafford Hundred (for the shopping centre) and Grays. And that is all. It might be added that 20 trains leave Fenchurch Street between 1700 and 1759 on Mondays to Fridays, which is another

Below: Unit No 321790 approaches Shadwell DLR station on 10 October 1995 with a down working to Shoeburyness. *John Glover*

measure of the peak period's domination.

Annual train miles are 3.1 million, with an average journey length of 19 miles. This brings in an average fare of £2.32 and a satisfactory average train loading of 132 passengers for a commuter railway. This will be helped by the importance of non-London destinations, such as Southend, Basildon and Barking for example; these and other stations have a considerable ability to attract both work and leisure traffic.

Trains, presently a mixed fleet of Classes 302, 310 and 312, are maintained at East Ham. All lines are electrified at 25kv ac.

Performance on reliability was 97.5% in 1994/95 (target 98.0%) and punctuality 87.7%, slightly below the 88.0% standard set.

The Tilbury has had its share of poor performance in recent years, with ageing signalling equipment and a 1960 build of trains both partially to blame. A further difficulty was the removal of LT&S tracks on the London side of Limehouse in order to accommodate the Docklands Light Railway. The infrastructure problems are now on their way to a satisfactory resolution; replacing the trains has to take account of the progress of new builds for other lines as well as the domestic problems of the LT&S.

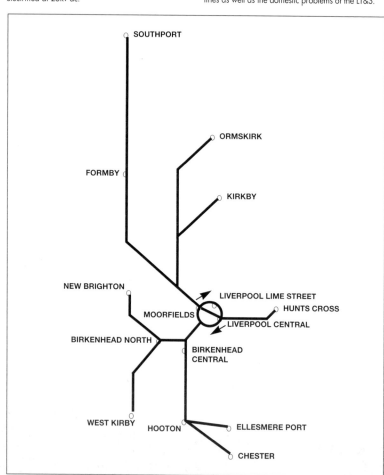

Merseyrail Electrics Ltd

The Merseyrail network has a variety of origins, the oldest part being the Mersey Railway which started electric working in 1903 between Liverpool Central and Rock Ferry. It was not until 1977/78 though that the 'loop and link' tunnelling scheme to unite the then electrified network under central Liverpool was completed, with the help of Merseyside PTE (Merseytravel). This brought together the lines to, respectively, Rock Ferry, West Kirby and New Brighton (the Wirral Lines, with a loop) and to Southport, Ormskirk and Kirkby, plus the reopened line to Garston (the link).

The system, electrified at 750v dc, was subsequently extended. Electrification reached Hunt's Cross (1983), Hooton (1985), Chester (1993) and Ellesmere Port (1994).

The service pattern is intense, with a 15min frequency standard on all routes. In the central area of Liverpool and including the section under the river between James Street and Hamilton Square, the combined service reaches 12tph or a train every 5min. The 15min frequency falls to 30min only for the two sections beyond Hooton, where Chester and Ellesmere Port each have a 2tph service. On the link line, the Southport trains are the ones projected to Hunt's Cross; the Kirkby and Ormskirk services terminate at Liverpool Central. Peak supplementation is confined to the Hooton line, where services are broadly doubled.

This concentrated operation provides the same number of annual train miles as on the LT&S at 3.1 million, but the average passenger journey length is only seven miles. Fares income equates to £0.90 per journey. Average train occupation is 47.

The service is provided by the (almost) identical Class 507 and 508 units and built around 1979.

These fleets are based at Hall Road and Birkenhead North respectively.

Reliability at 98.5% for 1994/95 was slightly below the standard of 99.0% and punctuality was also rather less good than it might have been at 89.5% against a 90.0% target.

What of the future? The railway depends on Liverpool at least as much as Liverpool depends on the railway; the fortunes of one affect the other. The recent prolonged closure of the city centre rail tunnel due to the problems of the rising water table must have been relatively disastrous for the Merseyrail business, quite apart from its effect on the city transport system. Such problems have to be overcome without service withdrawal wherever possible; if passengers are forced to find alternatives, some at least will stay with them.

Further system expansion may be possible, provided that this does not overload the present infrastructure. The trains which presently terminate at Liverpool Central could be extended eastwards beyond Hunt's Cross to Widnes and perhaps Warrington Central; another possibility would be to revive the Edge Hill spur proposal, for which a header tunnel was built at Central in the 1970s, to offer a service to St Helens Central. But these are not short-term schemes. They involve varying amounts of civil engineering work and electrification. Then, 25kv ac and dual voltage stock, or continue with 750v dc?

Below: **A St Pancras–Sheffield IC125 service with power car No 43051 leading at Kempston, south of Bedford, on 19 April 1989. The conveyor in the foreground is associated with the brick-making industry.** *John Glover*

INTERCITY
Midland Main Line

LEEDS
SHEFFIELD — DONCASTER
DERBY — NOTTINGHAM
LEICESTER
BEDFORD
LONDON
ST PANCRAS

Midland Main Line Ltd

The Midland Railway was based in Derby, and in the company's mind everything radiated from there. For many years, in defiance of normal conventions, it was 'up' to Derby on the Midland, not to London.

The Midland Main Line is presently the only railway operator using St Pancras, which has a sadly deserted air about it as a result. IC125 sets provide all the services; every hour on the hour there is a train from St Pancras to Nottingham and on the half hour to Sheffield via Derby. Leicester has the benefit of being served by both. In the busiest hours the number of departures rises to four.

There is some origination of early services from north of Sheffield, since the 14 IC125 sets are all based at Neville Hill, Leeds. There is a similar extension of trains north of Sheffield in the evenings. Thus, the 1820 St Pancras to Nottingham train reverses at Nottingham, to proceed via Alfreton (now shorn of its Parkway status) to Sheffield. It then runs via Doncaster and Wakefield Westgate to Leeds. Other services omit the Doncaster detour.

This is a limited operation and the annual train miles of 3.1m are the same as both Merseyrail Electrics and the LT&S. Journey length is much higher at an average 80 miles (London to Market Harborough). This elicits a revenue of £11.35, putting the Midland Main Line behind only the East and West Coast InterCity companies. Average occupancy of the trains is 134 passengers. Leisure is

recorded as the principal market, but business travel is also significant. There is also some commuting, notably from Leicester southwards to London, but also into Leicester itself.

The service quality measurement saw reliability of 99.2% for 1994/95 (target 99.0%) and punctuality at 90.3% against 90.0%.

Like other IC125 users, the question mark over their lifespans grows increasingly bigger. Does electrification, already in place for the first 50 miles to Bedford, have any appeal as part of an investment strategy? What other alternatives will there be?

Of perhaps more immediate consequence is the forthcoming use of St Pancras as the CTRL London terminal. This will permit easy interchange into Midland Main Line trains, and slightly less easier transfer to neighbouring King's Cross. It will also be made possible to access the WCML out of Euston for the provision of direct services. Of these three routes, it is the Midland which, conspicuously, is not electrified. While this does not in any sense prohibit interchange, there may be a market for direct European services from Midland territory. For that, electrification would be a necessary requirement.

Little of the above concerns the Midland Main Line business in the short term, but pity the writer of the OPRAF Passenger Service Requirement.

Network SouthCentral Ltd

This highly complex series of lines is largely that bequeathed to present generations by the London Brighton and South Coast Railway. There are two distinct parts: the web of inner suburban services which form collectively the South London lines, and the longer distance operations out to the Sussex Coast. Both are made more difficult to comprehend by the width of London which confronts a railway approaching from due south, in that no single terminus can serve adequately both the City and the West End. Network SouthCentral's trains thus make either for the Brighton side terminal platforms at London Bridge (for the City) or for the Brighton side platforms at Victoria (for the West End).

As a further variation, a few Network SouthCentral trains cross to the South Eastern lines at London Bridge, to terminate eventually at Charing Cross. There is now a Charing Cross to Horsham service.

On the South London lines, most services operate at 30min headways. There are a few exceptions; Wimbledon–West Croydon runs every 45min so that it can be maintained with one train, the Tattenham Corner branch is only hourly beyond Smitham, and

Network SouthCentral

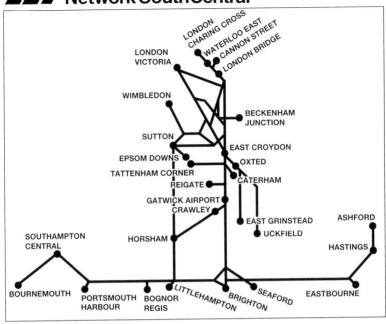

so on. On the other hand, stations from West Croydon to Sutton enjoy two 30min services, one from London Bridge and the other from Victoria, offering a 15min frequency.

Further south, frequencies tend to be nearer to hourly, whether on the non-electrified Uckfield branch from Oxted, or on services from London to the coastal routes, apart from Brighton itself. Thus, the following service pattern is provided every hour by Network SouthCentral:

- Victoria via Gatwick Airport to Lewes, Eastbourne and Hastings.
- Victoria via Gatwick Airport to Hove, Worthing (train divides). To Barnham, Havant, Fareham, Southampton Central and Bournemouth, and to Littlehampton.
- Victoria via the Arun Valley to Barnham (train divides). To Havant and Portsmouth Harbour, and to Bognor Regis.

The local service along the coast supplements this:

- Hastings, Eastbourne, Lewes, Brighton
- Eastbourne, Lewes, Brighton, West Worthing
- Seaford, Lewes, Brighton, Worthing, Littlehampton
- Seaford, Lewes
- Brighton, Worthing, Barnham, Havant, Portsmouth Harbour
- Littlehampton, Barnham, Bognor Regis
- Barnham, Bognor Regis

Omission of other station names is purely to simplify the illustration. The net effect is that many more journeys are possible without change of train, particularly across Brighton.

Another innovation is the three times daily Brighton to Ashford service, which supplements the hourly local Ashford-Hastings diesel units.

Long distance services rely on the ageing 4CIG and 4VEP units; these are allocated to Brighton. Local services are mostly in the hands of Class 455 or 456 units of more recent years. Class 319 ac/dc units of 1987 are also leased to Network SouthCentral, being surplus to Thameslink's current requirements. All are based at Selhurst, as are the few diesel units still required by Network SouthCentral.

Network SouthCentral is one of the larger TOCs, with 13.0 million train miles operated per year. It

71

does, however, have considerable volumes of short distance traffic, with a 15-mile average journey length for which the passenger pays £1.96. Average occupancy rate is 91 passengers; all of these statistics are very much in line with those of the other ex-Southern Region companies. NSC operates in busy commuting territory, but other traffic includes that to and from Gatwick and the attractions of Brighton.

Service reliability was over 99% for both service groups (South London Lines and Sussex Coast), targets 98.0% and 99.0% respectively, but punctuality was less satisfactory. For South London it was 90.8% against a target of 89.0%; for Sussex Coast a miserable 84.0% against an undemanding target of 85.0%.

As always with any commuter railway, its fortunes depend so much on the state of the local economy. Spare line capacity is available at present, but a return to 1989 levels could offer a few problems.

There are always new ideas to be tried, and the example of the Hastings to Portsmouth corridor shows some interesting innovations. The next task is to make sense for the average man in the street of the complex South London local services.

North London Railways Ltd

25kv ac electrification of the WCML to Euston in 1966 at last brought a quality outer suburban service to the communities north of Watford, which for years had endured irregularly spaced trains with gaps of up to nearly 3hr in the services from Euston to stations south of Bletchley.

Today, Milton Keynes Central is the terminus of a regular 30min North London Railways service calling at Harrow & Wealdstone, Watford Junction and all stations. A further 30min service calls intermediately at Watford Junction, Hemel Hempstead, Berkhamsted, Leighton Buzzard and Bletchley, but continues to Northampton and, with alternate trains only, to Birmingham New Street. The peak service more than doubles this service frequency.

And then there are the seven 'other' lines, whose total length is about equal to the distance between London and Rugby. These are discussed in turn.

- Euston, Willesden Junction, Harrow & Wealdstone and Watford Junction   17.75 miles

Below: **One of the last strongholds of Modernisation Plan dmus has been the Clapham Junction–Willesden Junction service. Class 117 power twin unit No 117001 forms the 1003 departure from Clapham Junction on 23 May 1995.** *John Glover*

This, the so-called 'New Line' from its construction in the early years of this century and subsequent 1922 electrification, offers a basic three trains per hour. These are supplemented by the projection of London Underground Bakerloo Line services from their usual Queen's Park terminus to Stonebridge Park or, occasionally, to Harrow & Wealdstone. Both systems are dc, but the fourth rail no longer extends beyond Harrow.

● Richmond, Willesden Junction, Gospel Oak,
  Stratford and North Woolwich   22.5 miles

A 4tph service is provided, albeit that single track beyond Custom House limits the frequency between Stratford and North Woolwich to 2tph. Electrification varies between fourth rail dc for the District Line sharing into Richmond, and third rail generally. However, 25kv ac is provided for freight between Camden Road and the Stratford area. From mid-1996, this is extended via Gospel Oak to South Acton for Eurostar purposes, with the third rail removed. This requires the use of the dual-voltage Class 313 units which presently operate these services and also those of the New Line and the Croxley Green branch. These two

lines form the core of today's inner suburban operations.

● Willesden Junction and Clapham Junction
                                    6.25 miles

This recently introduced 2tph service also requires Class 313 units, due to the change from overhead to third rail at the entrance to the Eurostar North Pole International Depot.

● Watford Junction and Croxley Green 2.75 miles

With but a residual service of one Class 313 per day on the 3rd rail, this line might yet become part of a Metropolitan line route to Watford Junction via the proposed Croxley link.

● Watford Junction and St Albans Abbey
                                    6.5 miles

Electrified at 25kv ac, this line has seen stations added at Garston and then How Wood. This is one train operation at a 45min headway, to suit the single journey time of 17min. There are no through workings off the branch.

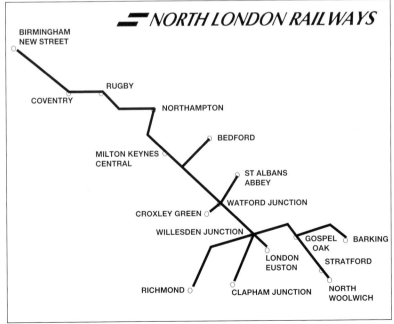

NORTH LONDON RAILWAYS

BIRMINGHAM
NEW STREET

RUGBY
COVENTRY
                    NORTHAMPTON

                              BEDFORD

MILTON KEYNES
CENTRAL
                    ST ALBANS
                    ABBEY
                    WATFORD JUNCTION
CROXLEY GREEN
        WILLESDEN JUNCTION
                                GOSPEL   BARKING
                                OAK
                    LONDON   STRATFORD
                    EUSTON

RICHMOND   CLAPHAM JUNCTION   NORTH
                                    WOOLWICH

- Gospel Oak and Barking   12.25 miles
- Bletchley and Bedford   16.75 miles

These two lines, one urban and one largely rural, remain outside the electrified network. They are condemned as a result to services provided by first generation dmus of Class 117, or the occasional Class 121 single unit. Services are half-hourly and hourly respectively. Traffic on both may euphemistically be described as 'light'.

North London Railways run 5.6 million train miles a year, while the average passenger journey length is 14 miles. This is worth £1.72 in operator income. Average occupancy is 78, close to the BR TOC average.

The fleet of both diesel and electric multiple units is allocated to Bletchley.

The Northampton lines performed reasonably well for service reliability at 98.4% for 1994/95, albeit that they were missing the target of 99.0%, but punctuality was only 87.3% as against a target of 90.0%. The North London lines were less satisfactory. Reliability was 95.6% compared with the target of 97.0%, while punctuality was 86.8% against a rather modest aim of 87.0%.

It is part of Railtrack's remit to carry out infrastructure work needed by train operators, such as European Passenger Services' requirements for their north of London trains. However, it is sad to record the resulting closure of the railway for many months in 1995/96 between Willesden Junction and Camden Road, with North London line trains diverted via Primrose Hill. This was not accompanied by the provision of any special facilities at all for the stations West Hampstead, Finchley Road & Frognal and Hampstead Heath. It might be asked, though, that if service usage is so low that passengers are deemed to be able to do without it for that length of time, is there any need to restore it subsequently? Or, alternatively, are there more profitable traffics from other operators, which Railtrack might carry instead?

On a more positive note, the further expansion of Milton Keynes may be hoped to bring further traffic to North London Railways, though some of this will be shared with InterCity West Coast. In the Department of Transport's view, Watford, Milton Keynes and Northampton are all important business centres attracting significant off-peak travel, but there are few tourist attractions in this route's corridor.

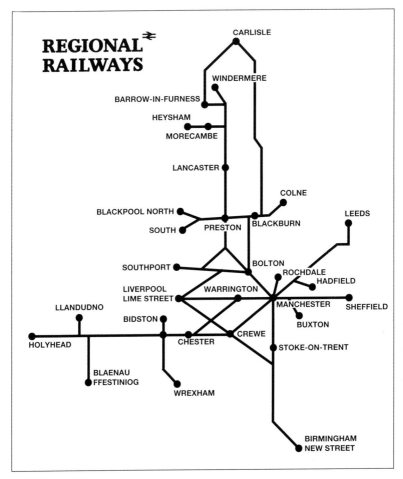

REGIONAL RAILWAYS

CARLISLE
WINDERMERE
BARROW-IN-FURNESS
HEYSHAM
MORECAMBE
LANCASTER
COLNE
BLACKPOOL NORTH
LEEDS
SOUTH
PRESTON
BLACKBURN
BOLTON
SOUTHPORT
ROCHDALE
HADFIELD
LIVERPOOL
LIME STREET
WARRINGTON
LLANDUDNO
MANCHESTER
SHEFFIELD
BIDSTON
BUXTON
HOLYHEAD
CREWE
CHESTER
STOKE-ON-TRENT
BLAENAU
FFESTINIOG
WREXHAM
BIRMINGHAM
NEW STREET

North West Regional Railways Ltd

The core of North West Regional Railways' operating area is the complex network of railways surrounding Manchester and Liverpool. Built primarily by the London & North Western and the Lancashire &

Left: The 1123 Preston–Ormskirk service is formed of unit No 142045 on departure from Preston on 17 September 1993. *John Glover*

Yorkshire companies, but with generous contributions from (what became) the Great Central and others, unification was never the name of the game. However, in the last decade, two important linking pieces of infrastructure have been built, and another major traffic source can now be reached by rail. These are as follows:

● The Hazel Grove chord, which allows trains from Sheffield via the Hope Valley to enter Manchester via Stockport, and to continue via Oxford Road if required with minimal obstruction of the station throat at Piccadilly.

- The 700m Windsor Link, which allows trains from Manchester Oxford Road to gain access to the L&Y lines from Manchester Victoria towards Bolton, at a new Salford Crescent station.

- The opening of Manchester Airport station, connected initially by a facing junction to the Styal line towards Manchester, but with a south-facing junction towards Crewe added subsequently.

It might also be added that some conventional rail traffic was lost with the acquisition of the Bury and Altrincham branches for Metrolink. Nevertheless, the advent of these schemes has allowed a complete rethink of the means of serving Greater Manchester by rail, amongst which has been the substantial downgrading of Victoria station.

North West Regional Railways (NWRR) is the principal operator, whose interests stretch from Holyhead to the Cumbrian Coast, as well as the land east of the Pennines. Services may be divided into urban services, mostly the subject of s20 agreements with Greater Manchester PTE or Merseytravel; longer distance services; and rural. Of these, the urban services are understood to account for well over half of NWRR's total revenue.

The PTE diesel services in Merseyside and all local services in the Manchester area are run to PTE specifications. Service frequencies are often 2tph or more, especially when several services run between the same points — as, for instance, between Manchester and Romiley.

The longer distance services, mostly hourly, include:

- Crewe–Holyhead (with an interspersed service to Chester only)
- Manchester Oxford Road–Llandudno
- Liverpool Lime Street–Preston–Morecambe
- Manchester Airport, Piccadilly, Stockport, Sheffield, Doncaster, Cleethorpes
- Manchester Airport, Piccadilly, Bolton, Preston, Blackpool North
- As above to Preston, then continuing to Barrow-in-Furness, Windermere or Carlisle

The truly rural services include those between Llandudno and Blaenau Ffestiniog; Barrow-in-Furness, Whitehaven and Carlisle; and Oxenholme Lake District and Windermere. Services such as Preston-Ormskirk also perhaps come into this category. These routes are typified by the use of minimum resources to provide a service, the intervals

of which often appear to owe as much to economical rostering of staff and diesel units as to passenger demand.

A feature of recent years has been the growth of longer distance urban services, longer in the sense of end-to-end journey times and distances rather than any noticeable affinity between the places at either end. Some of those operated by NWRR, all hourly, are:

- Southport and Chester
  30 stations   83 miles   158 min
- Buxton and Blackpool North
  27 stations   75 miles   137 min
- Blackpool South and Colne
  26 stations   50 miles   109 min
- Shaw & Crompton and Clitheroe
  20 stations   44 miles   106 min
- Rochdale and Wigan Wallgate
  12 stations   33 miles   70 min

It takes little work with a calculator to show, at around a 30mph average speed, how tedious such journeys are over longer distances. They may minimise the use of land in city centres and be cheap to provide, but such operations hardly show the railway at its best.

The NWRR diesel unit fleet is a mixture of Class 142 Pacers and heavier duty dmus of Classes 150, 153 and 156, plus some Class 158s. The principal maintenance depot is Newton Heath. Class 323 electric units are now superseding the Modernisation Plan Class 304s and 308s.

North West Regional Railways run a sizeable 14.0 million train miles a year, with an average passenger journey length of 17 miles. The associated revenue per journey is £2.00. Usage, however, in terms of train occupancy, is depressingly low, with only 27 persons at a time on the average train. Might this have something to do with service performance? By area, NWRR's 1994/95 results were as follows; all were worse than in the previous year:

It is acknowledged that the Charter punctuality

Right: **Forming a Liverpool Lime Street–Newcastle trans-Pennine service, three-car Class 158/0 No 158801 passes the site of Dearness Valley Junction, Relly Mill, Durham, on a sunny 23 February 1995.**
Brian Morrison

Area	Reliability	Target	Punctuality	Target
Cumbria	98.9%	99.0%	96.4%	90.0%
Lancashire local	97.7%	99.0%	87.4%	90.0%
Manchester local	97.8%	99.0%	84.1%	90.0%
Manchester long distance	97.5%	99.0%	91.2%	90.0%
North Wales branches	98.6%	99.0%	81.5%	90.0%
North Wales inter-urban	98.3%	99.0%	91.7%	90.0%

targets may be met more easily if some judicious adjustments are made to schedules. But, whatever the reason, such results do give credence to the dissatisfaction expressed by the Greater Manchester Passenger Transport Authority and their withdrawal in April 1996 from the s20 funding arrangement, by which means the PTE elements of service provision are supported.

However, assuming happier times in the future, there remains much to do in the area. The growing Manchester Airport originates a 5tph service northwards, but there are more potential destinations than there are train paths. In infrastructure terms, the congested link from Slade Green Junction (at the northern end of the Styal line), through Piccadilly to Oxford Road and Deansgate is perhaps the most restrictive element, but what other use might be made of further airport connections?

There are other TOCs in the area who might well offer some competition, while electrification of any part or all of the trans-Pennine route via Huddersfield, the missing elements of the line from Manchester through to Preston (or Blackpool North), or more lines east of Liverpool Lime Street would again alter the range of services which might be provided.

Meanwhile, how might services in the Blackburn and Burnley areas be developed most effectively?

77

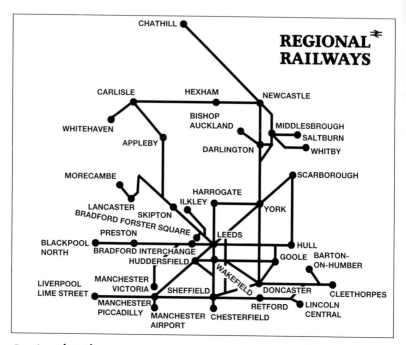

Regional Railways North East Ltd

Regional Railways North East cover the whole of the Yorkshire area and northwards almost to the Border. Also within the area, of course, are the two InterCity companies of East Coast and Cross Country, while Regional Railways North West and Central Trains lie to the west and south respectively.

Historically, the north east was a one-company area, the grip of the North Eastern Railway being well known. Further south, the Midland penetrated to West Yorkshire, as did some companies from Lancashire, but the network complexities resulting from rival schemes have long been all but eliminated. It is now nearly 30 years since Leeds and Sheffield each had more than one station.

There are a number of long distance services operated by Regional Railways North East (RRNE). These include the following hourly services, which together provide a 3tph fast service between Leeds and Manchester:

● Newcastle, York, Leeds, Huddersfield, Manchester Piccadilly and Liverpool Lime Street.

Alternately, these trains start from Scarborough.
● Middlesbrough, York, Leeds, Huddersfield, Manchester Piccadilly and Manchester Airport.
● Hull, Leeds, Huddersfield and Manchester Piccadilly.

Other hourly services include:

● York, Leeds, Bradford Interchange, Burnley, Preston and Blackpool North.
● York, Leeds, Bradford Interchange, Hebden Bridge and Manchester Victoria. Alternately, these trains start from Selby.
● (Middlesbrough), Sunderland, Newcastle, Hexham, (Carlisle).
● Wakefield Westgate, Huddersfield and Manchester Victoria.

And, at about a two-hourly frequency:

● Leeds, Skipton, Carnforth and Morecambe.
● Leeds, Skipton, Settle and Carlisle.
● Saltburn, Middlesbrough, Darlington, Durham and Newcastle.
● Saltburn, Middlesbrough, Darlington and Bishop Auckland.

The latter are additional to the hourly local Saltburn to Darlington service.

RRNE provide urban services for three PTEs: West Yorkshire (METRO), South Yorkshire and Tyne & Wear. Tyne & Wear's only s20 service is that between Newcastle and Sunderland (4tph), while South Yorkshire's involvement has always been limited, due to the relatively small part of the railway system which lies within its boundaries. All lines heading northwards to Leeds have a joint involvement with METRO.

Leeds is in many ways the centre of the network. From here, local electric services now reach to Wakefield Westgate plus Doncaster (1tph, but 2tph from Adwick into Doncaster), while Ilkley and Skipton each have trains at 2tph from both Bradford Forster Square and Leeds. This gives a 15min service to each of those destinations!

Diesel units from Leeds offer 2tph to Harrogate and Knaresborough, one of which continues to York. An important service is that to Castleford, Wakefield Kirkgate, Barnsley and Sheffield. Hourly from Leeds, it becomes 2tph from Wakefield Kirkgate and 3tph from Barnsley with the addition of a train from Huddersfield via Penistone. Sheffield may also be reached via Moorthorpe.

Other services of interest to SYPTE include 4tph from Sheffield to Doncaster, one of which continues to Hull and another (ex-Manchester Airport) to Cleethorpes. Over the old Great Central network there is a 1tph service to Worksop and Retford, alternate services continuing to Lincoln.

Elsewhere on the network, Regional Railways North East run hourly between Scunthorpe and Doncaster and between Wakefield Westgate and Pontefract Monkhill. Hull to Bridlington has 2tph, reducing to 1tph or less thence to Scarborough. And while there is an hourly service from Newcastle to Morpeth, the service thence to Chathill is a once or twice a day residual operation.

Other very limited services are those on alternate hours between Cleethorpes and Barton-on-Humber,

the very occasional projections beyond Knottingley to Goole, York to Hull via Selby trains, the residual Sheffield to York direct, and the poor old Whitby branch from Middlesbrough. One has the distinct impression that these are very much grant-induced services.

This is not a complete inventory; one-off services such as the 1600 weekdays Sunderland to Whitehaven service always provoke a degree of incredulity, but they really do exist.

How do Regional Railways North East compare with others? RRNE operate as many as 18.0m train miles a year and the average passenger journey length is 20 miles — but for a fare of only £1.79. On the other hand, the average train occupancy rate at 38 matches that of Central Trains, with whose operation that of RRNE is perhaps broadly comparable.

Rolling stock, a variety of Class 14x units and the more salubrious Class 15x diesel units are maintained at Neville Hill (Leeds) or Heaton (Newcastle). Some of these units are owned by METRO, albeit that they are managed by Porterbrook Leasing Co Ltd. Electric units comprise a small Class 321 fleet and some Class 308s drafted in for the Airedale and Wharfedale electrification.

On performance, the trans-Pennine services appear to be the least satisfactory (See table below). Of new developments in the area, both Meadowhall and Gateshead Metro Centre are out of town shopping centres which are reasonably close to an RRNE station. Clearly, RRNE could obtain considerable advantage from the implementation of trans-Pennine electrification, especially if extended at the eastern end to York and perhaps also to Hull.

Infrastructure problems include the Leeds area station layout and its signalling, both of which were essentially designed for rather lower rail traffic levels. And therein lies one of the principal benefits which local railways can bring: the relief of road congestion in urban areas. What is the best way to make use of this opportunity?

Area	Reliability	Target	Punctuality	Target
Northern long distance	98.1%	99.0%	94.9%	90.0%.
Northern short distance	97.5%	99.0%	91.3%	90.0%.
South Yorks & Humberside long	98.4%	99.0%	94.1%	90.0%.
South Yorks & Humberside short	98.8%	99.0%	92.2%	90.0%.
Trans-Pennine	97.7%	99.0%	89.7%	90.0%.
West Yorkshire long distance	98.4%	99.0%	93.8%	90.0%.
West Yorkshire short distance	98.7%	99.0%	91.8%	90.0%.

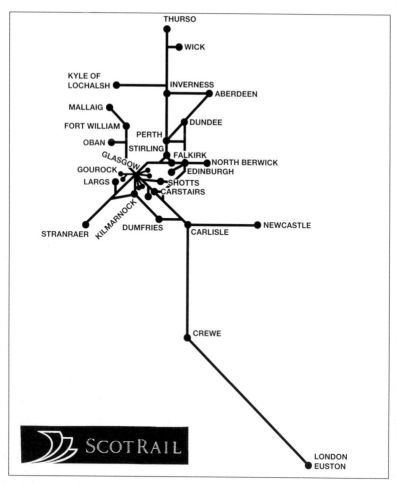

ScotRail Railways Ltd

ScotRail TOC is the nearest reached to a self-contained railway system on mainland Britain. Although InterCity companies in the form of East Coast, West Coast and Cross Country all penetrate on occasion as far as Glasgow Central, Inverness and Aberdeen, ScotRail is largely its own master. Indeed, since assuming control of the Anglo-Scottish sleeper services, it has a toehold all the way to London via the West Coast route.

Strathclyde PTE has the largest urban network outside London and is correspondingly important to ScotRail as a source of revenue and of business. The heart of Strathclyde's Glasgow operation is that of the former 'Blue Trains', the electrics which plied the network from 1960. The 'north side' electric services, as joined subsequently by the Argyle line services to the southeast, are displayed in Table 226 of the timetable. Suffice to say here that this whole network operates on a basic half-hourly frequency, save only the section beyond Motherwell to Lanark, and that this equates to 6tph through Glasgow Queen Street low level and 4tph through Central low level. Partick, where both lines join and which has interchange with the Glasgow Underground, has a splendid 10tph off-peak service.

However, life is never quite so simple; flooding on the Argyle line led to its prolonged closure for nine months in 1995, during which time the service had to be suspended.

Although not in the London category of size, Glasgow stretches a considerable distance for its catchment. Typically, cross-Glasgow journeys like Drumgelloch to Helensburgh, or Lanark to Milngavie are 35 miles or so in length, similar to the distance between Croydon and Stevenage. The 2tph frequency extends also to the 'south side' services which make up the Cathcart circle group, to Ayr, Ardrossan and to Gourock, though Largs and Wemyss Bay each have only an hourly service.

Diesel services, such as to Cumbernauld, Maryhill, Paisley Canal, East Kilbride and Barrhead are also at 2tph, though services to Kilmarnock are hourly.

Edinburgh's suburban services are much more limited; electric trains to North Berwick run hourly, as does the Bathgate service. The Fife circle to Dunfermline and Kirkcaldy runs hourly in each direction. The local service to Glasgow Central via Shotts is also hourly.

Longer distance services include that between Edinburgh and Glasgow Queen Street via Falkirk High, presently 2tph but prospectively 4tph. The main alternative is of course to travel InterCity via Carstairs to Central.

Both Glasgow Queen Street and Edinburgh offer an hourly service to Aberdeen, which gives 2tph north of Dundee. Of the eight daily Inverness services, Edinburgh has the majority, but other connections are available at Perth.

In the Highlands, Oban, Mallaig, Kyle of Lochalsh and the Far North line to Wick all survive on a basic three trains per day service. Wick can now be reached only via Thurso, adding a 13-mile round trip and half an hour to the journey times. Intrepid passengers for Wick may, of course, disembark at Georgemas Junction to admire the scenery while their train runs up to Thurso and back again. The Aberdeen–Elgin–Inverness service runs alternate hours.

Below: On 3 September 1993, Class 320 No 320313 stops at Glasgow Queen Street Low Level, while forming the 1524 Helensburgh Central–Airdrie. *Brian Morrison*

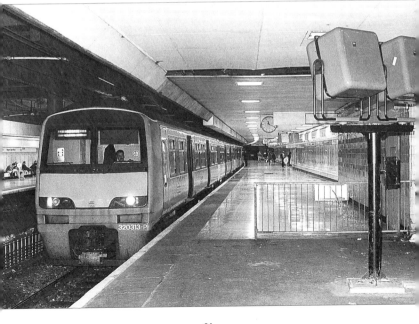

An interesting development is that associated with the former Glasgow & South Western routes. From Glasgow Central, both to Carlisle and to Stranraer, services run about every 2hr.

It is now possible to catch ScotRail's 1237 'Galloway Enterprise' from Newcastle to Stranraer, via Carlisle, Kilmarnock and Troon, to be deposited there 230 miles and 5hr 23min later at a 42mph average speed. This leaves an hour to steady oneself and make ready for the 1900 short sea crossing to Larne, arriving in Northern Ireland at 2120. The train thence to Belfast Central arrives at 2234.

There are other direct links from Scotland to the Newcastle–Carlisle line, some of which are geared to give access to the Gateshead Metro Centre station.

ScotRail's fleet consists of a handful of first generation diesel units of Classes 101 and 117, while the remainder is formed from Classes 150, 156 and 158. These are maintained at Haymarket and Corkerhill. The 25kv ac electric units are of Class 303 (the original Blue Trains), 305 (brought in for North Berwick electrification), 314 (Argyle line), 318 (Ayrshire electrification) and 320 (Class 321 clones). These are maintained at Glasgow Shields and at Yoker. Locomotives and coaching stock, including sleeping cars, are based and maintained at Inverness.

As a business, ScotRail tops the list of BR TOCs with 19.0m train miles a year. Even so, the average passenger journey length is no more than 17 miles, which perhaps represents the importance of the urban services in general and in Strathclyde in particular as a proportion of the total. Revenue per journey is also relatively low at £1.76. The average passenger occupancy per train is also well down at 45.

In performance terms, while reliability is above target, punctuality clearly leaves something to be desired, both in the Central and East areas:

Area	Reliability	Target	Punctuality	Target
Central	99.1%	99.0%	86.2%	90.0%
East	99.3%	99.0%	85.2%	90.0%
Express	99.5%	99.0%	91.2%	90.0%
Highland	99.7%	99.0%	92.7%	90.0%
South West	99.5%	99.0%	93.2%	90.0%

Unit No 158.718 forms the 1210 Edinburgh–Aberdeen as it arrives at Ladybank on 11 November 1995.
Martin Higginson

The development of ScotRail's Edinburgh-Glasgow Queen Street via Falkirk High service has already been touched upon. There are also a number of infrastructure investments under consideration, such as Glasgow's CrossRail north to south link over a reinvigorated Tron line, now freight only. Electrification of additional parts of the network, notably to Aberdeen, would also make a different range of service options possible. Around Aberdeen itself, there is some pressure from Grampian Regional Council for a local service to be reinstated.

Particularly in the Central Lowlands, there is little spare railway capacity, which would make real competition difficult to achieve. So, the railway must meet the needs of its passengers as best it can, economically and with regard to local transport planning aspirations. Who better to express these than bodies like Strathclyde PTE (who have to back their decisions with funding) and Lothian Regional Council, or their successors?

The South Eastern Train Co Ltd

The South Eastern Train Co carries a very sizeable passenger traffic; in many ways it is the county of Kent's rail operator, at least for domestic traffic.

The network over which today's South Eastern operate still bears the scars of the 19th century clashes between the established and staid South Eastern Railway and the brash newcomer of the London, Chatham and Dover Railway. Historians refer to the inter-company relations as 'the feud'. Despite the efforts of the Southern Railway and subsequently British Railways modernisation plan works, such as the junctions at Chislehurst, it remains a complex network.

The London termini served are Charing Cross, Cannon Street, Blackfriars and Victoria. As with Network SouthCentral's services, this was a consequence of companies wanting access both to the City and the West End. However, here there were two companies who were each trying to do this.

Today's inner suburban services revolve around a 30min headway. From Charing Cross, on the mid-Kent line, there is a 2tph service to Hayes, with shuttle connections for Addiscombe. This is superimposed, in part, by a Cannon Street–Orpington 1tph service.

Further east, there is another 1tph Cannon Street–Orpington service, but this time on the main line via Elmstead Woods. This is interwoven with a 2tph Charing Cross to Orpington stopping service,

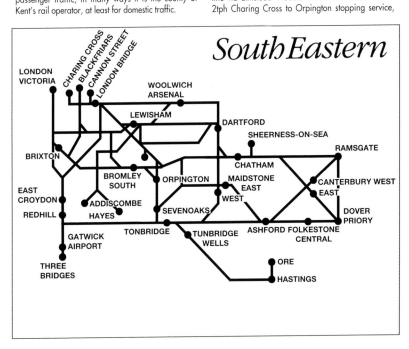

Below: Networker trains now monopolise the inner-suburban services. Seen here on 11 November 1995 at Waterloo East is unit No 465166 on a Charing Cross-bound train. *John Glover*

one of which continues to Sevenoaks. Bromley North is served by a 2tph shuttle from Grove Park, which appears to connect with nothing in particular.

Also, 2tph depart from Charing Cross for Dartford over each of the three routes, via Greenwich, via Kidbrooke and via Sidcup respectively. Alone, the Kidbrooke service is extended to Gravesend. Additionally, from Cannon Street there are 2tph on short journeys to Plumstead, and 1tph to Sidcup only. From Victoria, there are an additional 2tph via Kidbrooke to Dartford. On top of all this, there is a semi-fast 2tph Charing Cross to Gillingham service, which has a 2tph connection from Strood to Maidstone West.

There are few inner services on the Chatham side, but these include a 2tph Victoria to Orpington service via Kent House and 2tph from Blackfriars via Catford to Sevenoaks.

If the service patterns seem desperately complicated, then that is probably because they are so. Take the case of Orpington; a 9tph service sounds very respectable but, in reality, this is made up of 5tph from Charing Cross, 2tph from Cannon Street and 2tph from Victoria. What the travelling public makes of it is another matter; compare this necessarily abbreviated description with the relative simplicity of travelling by London Underground.

The longer distance services from Charing Cross via Tonbridge consist of 2tph to Hastings and 2tph to Ashford. These latter are extended to Dover Priory and Ramsgate respectively. But Tonbridge has two other hourly services, made possible by the electrification of the South Eastern line from Redhill. These are:

- Three Bridges–Gatwick Airport–Redhill, and all stations to Tonbridge, Paddock Wood and Maidstone West.
- Victoria–East Croydon-Redhill-Edenbridge-Tonbridge–High Brooms and Tunbridge Wells.

A journey time of 80min for the 40.75 miles between Gatwick and Maidstone is not perhaps record-breaking, but is nevertheless an interesting development, while Croydon is opened as both a business and a shopping centre for Tonbridge and Tunbridge Wells.

Maidstone East enjoys an hourly Charing Cross to Ashford and Ramsgate train and 2tph from Victoria, one of which is extended to Canterbury West.

The heart of the Chatham territory is the North Kent line from Bromley South via Chatham and Gillingham to Sittingbourne (2tph connections to Sheerness-on-Sea) and Faversham. From here, there is a choice of routes to Margate and Ramsgate, or to Canterbury East and Dover Priory. Hourly services, stopping at those stations, are provided to each branch. The Ramsgate trains split at Faversham to provide both fast and stopping services to Ramsgate, but in addition cross-platform connections into and out of a slow Victoria–Dover Priory service is provided from the fast Ramsgates and into and out of a slow Victoria–Ramsgate service from the fast Dover Priorys.

Annual train miles by The South Eastern Train Co are a sizeable 16.0 million, putting the company in the top echelon. Perhaps surprisingly, average passenger journey length is only 15 miles, bringing in £2.09; this may be an indication of the importance of the dense inner-suburban operation. An average train occupancy of 97 is encouraging.

All operations are over the electrified 750v dc network. A fleet of 97 four-car Class 465 and 43 Class 466 two-car Networker units provide the inner services from Slade Green, but the outer operations are still the preserve of the ageing Class 411 4-CEP Kent Coast Express stock. These date from around 1960 and are supplemented by some slightly newer Class 421 and 423 units. All these are based at Ramsgate. While a modest injection of Class 365 Networker Express units will help the situation, no comprehensive replacement policy has yet been concluded. The Class 365 fleet will offer hourly

Above: Dover Priory on 6 March 1993 sees Class 411/5 4-CEP stock No 1519 about to depart for the now closed Dover Western Docks. *John Glover*

services from Victoria to Ramsgate via Chatham and to Margate via Ashford.

The Kent Link inner services recorded service reliability at 98.6% for 1994/95 (target 98.0%), with punctuality at 88.1% against a target of 88.0%. Kent Coast's reliability was above the 99.0% target at 99.4%, but punctuality at 83.6% was very disappointing. The target was 82.0%. Punctuality was, however, slightly improved over 1993/94.

The inheritance of competing lines from the Victorian era still has its effects on service patterns, to which another new player is likely to be added. The Channel Tunnel Rail Link will be able to offer the capacity to carry 8tph at peak from both the Ashford and Northfleet (Ebbsfleet) areas; most, if not all, of these trains are likely to originate on the network presently served by South Eastern Trains.

This network is currently carrying both Eurostar passenger and also Channel Tunnel freight services, both of which represent an element of capacity constraint. On the other hand, this is offset by the loss of boat train traffic, which is much diminished from past years.

The East Thames corridor offers regeneration prospects, which might bring a new rail crossing of the Thames in the Woolwich Arsenal area. This could link north Kent with the North London Line. This has been canvassed as being able to offer services through to Stratford and perhaps beyond.

South Wales & West Railways Ltd

The West Country has always been a difficult area for rail, split between the Great Western and London & South Western companies, and without any real industrial base. In South Wales, all becomes very rural once Swansea has been passed.

In South Wales and West Railways' (SWWR) territory there are no PTEs, while the Cardiff Valleys have been hived off to another concern. There is thus much more emphasis on the inter-urban and rural operations. Indeed, urban work is confined to minor routes such as the hourly Severn Beach branch, the 2tph on the Exeter St Davids to Exmouth line and the recently introduced Cardiff Central to Maesteg and

Bridgend to Swansea services, both at 1tph.

Some inter-urban services are marketed under the Alphaline banner, which offers a Class 158 with trolley service and reservable seats:

- Cardiff Central, Bristol Temple Meads, Salisbury, Southampton Central and Portsmouth Harbour
- Cardiff Central, Hereford, Shrewsbury, Crewe and Manchester Piccadilly

Other services include:

- Bristol Temple Meads, Westbury and Weymouth

- Cardiff Central to Weston-super-Mare, some projected to Paignton, Plymouth or Penzance
- Swindon, Gloucester and Cheltenham Spa
- Swansea, Carmarthen, thence to Milford Haven or Pembroke Dock
- Bristol Temple Meads, Weston-super-Mare, some projected to Taunton
- Exeter Central to Barnstaple
- Exeter Central to Paignton
- Shrewsbury to Crewe
- Swansea, Llanelli, Llandrindod and Shrewsbury

But service frequencies are often low, with 1tph at

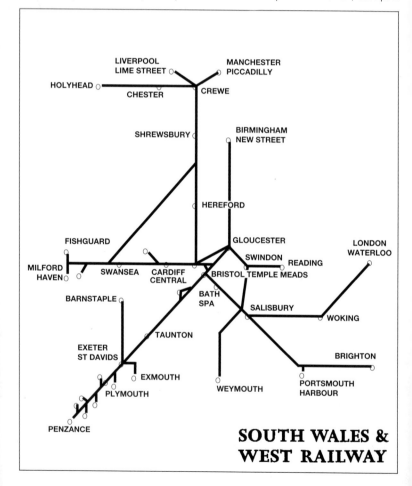

SOUTH WALES & WEST RAILWAY

Above: The capacious Bristol Temple Meads offers very adequate space for unit No 150230, which is about to form the 1130 departure to Gloucester on 27 July 1992. *John Glover*

best in this last group, and in the case of the Central Wales line, only trains per day.

Other limited services do run, such as the 0600 (weekdays) Carmarthen to Waterloo, in connection with Eurostar services, the 0945 Cardiff Central to Liverpool Lime Street (weekdays) and the 1500 (Sundays) Holyhead to Carmarthen.

Noticeably, there are only what might be termed 'fill-in' services by SWWR west of Plymouth, in the gaps left by Great Western or Cross Country InterCity services. Here, the main role of SWWR is to operate the five branches, whose Monday-to-Friday winter service is shown above right.

Service intervals are not regular, principally because of the importance of connecting with main line trains, in both directions if possible, at the junction for the branch. Most branches are effectively self-contained. The main exception is St Ives, where the unit makes alternate trips to and from Penzance rather than only to the junction station of St Erth.

- Plymouth and Gunnislake
  8 trains/day   14.75 miles   44min
- Liskeard and Looe
  9 trains/day   8.75 miles   25–30min
- Par to Newquay
  4 trains/day   20.75 miles   52min
- Truro to Falmouth
  13 trains/day   12.25 miles   22min
- St Erth to St Ives
  17 trains/day   4.25 miles   10–13min

At 11.0m, South Wales and West Railways operate as many train miles as do InterCity West Coast. With a substantial 34 miles as the average journey length, the fares changing hands are an above average £3.33. At 37 passenger miles per train mile, this measure is the same as Central Trains.

Services are operated by the usual mix of modern diesel units. This includes the Class 143 Pacer units used on the services sponsored by Mid-Glamorgan and West Glamorgan County Councils, and owned by them. Maintenance is carried out at Cardiff Canton.

Reliability is consistently slightly below target, but only in Avon did punctuality fail to reach the required level.

Area	Reliability	Target	Punctuality	Target
Avon	97.4%	99.0%	86.0%	90.0%
Cornwall	97.7%	99.0%	96.9%	90.0%
Devon	99.3%	99.0%	92.8%	90.0%
South Cotswolds	98.6%	99.0%	90.9%	90.0%
West and Central Wales	98.6%	99.0%	95.1%	90.0%
Western Inter-Urban	98.5%	99.0%	90.6%	90.0%

Much of the operation is clearly seasonal, which is a constraint in itself. However, the urban traffic problem remains, whether in the larger cities served by SWWR or the smaller ones. There is much to be gained by making the maximum use possible of an existing infrastructure to provide services into the towns of the area, and several station openings have been commissioned in recent years.

Perhaps the greater problem for SWWR is the priority which it can expect when train paths in areas like Bristol are being allocated and, in the more rural parts of its operating area, how its services should relate to those of the InterCity companies. Are main line connections more, or less, important than local travel needs? Whose business gains (or suffers)? Who is really in a position to resolve any insoluble differences of opinion, if there is no British Railways Board to bang heads together?

South West Trains Ltd

South West Trains (SWT) is in many ways still the London & South Western Railway, shorn of everything west of Exeter and a few branches. It still has the same uneasy relationship with the Brighton company in the east.

Today, the inner suburban services via Wimbledon virtually all run at 2tph, as indeed do the Windsor line services. The only exceptions are where 1tph stops short, such as the Waterloo to Weybridge service at Staines, or the 2tph fast Epsom services which are projected alternately to Horsham and Guildford.

In the outer suburban services there are similar effects, with one of the Alton services terminating at Farnham, and half the Guildford–Aldershot–Ascot service to Aldershot. But change is appearing, in that there are now two additional fast trains per hour between Ascot, Bracknell, Wokingham and Reading only. On the Portsmouth line, a 3tph service mix of fast, semi-fast and slow has an additional stopping train between Guildford and Haslemere only. On the West of England main line, departures are hourly, but some trains terminate short at Gillingham or Yeovil Junction, whereas a few are projected to Paignton.

Below: Wessex Express Class 442 stock No 2423 at Waterloo starts to move with the 0853 to Poole. *John Glover*

The Bournemouth line sees an hourly Weymouth and an hourly Poole, filled in by two stopping trains to Basingstoke only and other extras to serve intermediate stations and the Lymington Pier branch. Notable is the Winchester–Fareham–Portsmouth Harbour service via Botley.

Other railways use parts of the Bournemouth line, whether from Victoria and along the coast to Bournemouth as with Network SouthCentral, or to gain access from the Midlands like Cross Country trains. A recent innovation by SWT is a 1tph Brighton, Worthing, Havant, Winchester, Basingstoke service, which is continued on to Reading in alternate hours.

South West Trains runs an extensive service which requires a hefty 18.0m train miles a year. The intensity of suburban use is reflected in the 18-mile average journey length, worth £2.42 in passenger revenue. However, train occupancy rates at an average 58 people are relatively good.

Service provision is in the hands of Class 455 units for the inner services, and apart from the Class 442 Wessex Electrics, elderly CIG and VEP stock for the outer electric operations. The Exeter line has the Class 159s, based at their own Salisbury depot; electric stock is maintained at Wimbledon, Eastleigh, Fratton and Bournemouth.

Main line service reliability was 99.5%, better than the target 98.5%, but punctuality was 87.4% against a modest target of 87.0%. The suburban services achieved service reliability of 99.3% (target 99.0%) and punctuality was 91.2% against a target of 90.0%.

The indigenous commuter traffic for both inner and outer services is characterised by a mature and prosperous ABC1 market, while Haslemere has the highest number of first class season ticket holders in the country. Such, anyway, are the conclusions of the Department of Transport. One can almost hear the slamming of the doors on the VEP units.

Commuting is augmented by both business use and leisure traffic, with attractions such as Windsor Castle, Winchester, Salisbury and Portsmouth among the destinations reached. The railway also serves some major shopping centres at Guildford, Kingston and Southampton.

While SWT has launched a modest offensive against the Brighton in the Epsom–Leatherhead–Dorking–Horsham corridor, the Bournemouth line with its access to Reading seems more likely to produce new service patterns. Line capacity is one restraint; this particularly affects the number of trains which can access Waterloo at busy times.

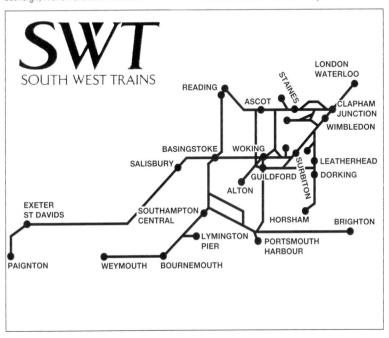

Heathrow Airport is also near to the line between Feltham, Ashford and Staines. There is, as they say, scope for a more productive rail involvement, with or without Terminal 5. Will South West Trains be a beneficiary?

Thames Trains Ltd

Thames Trains run at the London end of the Great Western main line, and make extensive use of the relief lines which continue as far as Didcot. This is not inner suburban traffic; the destinations served are as far afield as Bedwyn (66.50 miles from Paddington), Hereford (149.75 miles) and Stratford-upon-Avon (121.50 miles). These are sizeable distances, for which the high specification Class 165 series units are reasonably suitable.

The hourly service pattern from London is as follows:

- 2tph to Greenford, via Ealing Broadway
- 2tph all stations to Slough
- 2tph principal stations to Reading, alternately extended to Oxford
- 1tph stations to Bedwyn

Together with a 1tph all stations service from Reading to Oxford and 2tph Reading to Basingstoke, this covers most of the main line. There are also branches to Windsor & Eton Central (2tph) and Marlow (1tph), whose services are self-contained, and Henley-on-Thames (1tph), whose off-peak services run through to Reading.

A further group of services is those provided towards Gatwick Airport from Reading. An hourly fast service is supplemented with an hourly stopping service to Shalford, one station beyond Guildford. A further two hourly service calls at intermediate stations from Guildford to Redhill.

Thames Trains' long distance Turbo Express services leave Paddington at xx48; all proceed to Oxford. From there, successive trains in the midday period continue to Hereford, Banbury, Great Malvern and Stratford-upon-Avon. The last of these is a four per day service, and provides nearly half the trains over the Leamington Spa to Stratford-upon-Avon line. The last train back to Paddington leaves at the innovative time of 2315, arriving in the London terminus at 0129. Interestingly, on Saturdays, this service is provided by a bus which is actually 3min faster to Oxford, arriving at 0016, but gets into

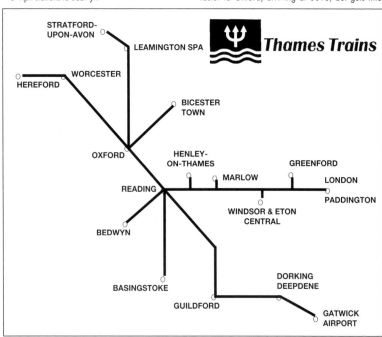

Above: The Oxford–Bicester Town service now amounts to 12 trips in each direction on weekdays and four on Sundays. Trains are allowed 26min for the 11.75 miles. The 1525 departure from Oxford, seen here on 3 October 1992, is formed of unit No 165123. *John Glover*

Paddington at an even more dismal 0225.

Thames Trains run a substantial 5.3 million train miles a year, with an average passenger journey length of 16 miles for which a fare of £1.92 is paid. The mean occupancy level is 71 passenger miles per train mile.

The Thames Trains fleet consists of a mix of two- and three-car Class 165/0 and 165/1 units, plus the Class 166 build of 21 three-car air-conditioned sets. All are based at Reading.

Service performance found reliability at 98.7% for 1994/95 (target 98.5%) and punctuality at 93.5% against an unexacting target of 85.0%.

The operator of a suburban service always has the opportunity to extend his geographical area of interest. Thus a Turbo Express to Hereford can be quite competitive in overall timings with an IC125 to Newport and changing trains there. Again, neither Bedwyn, Basingstoke nor Gatwick are at the ends of their respective lines.

On the other hand, Reading is accessed by other operators, who also provide services over links such as Basingstoke and Leamington Spa, and beyond at each end.

Perhaps the most interesting opportunities will come from new infrastructure investments. Potentially, three major developments are in the offing: first is the completion of the Heathrow Express Railway, especially if Terminal 5 is built and the severe capacity constraints anticipated in the short term within Heathrow can be alleviated; second are the possibilities represented by CrossRail and third the electrification and upgrading of the Great Western main line.

Thameslink Rail Ltd

Thameslink grew out of the foresight of the former Greater London Council, who commissioned a detailed study of the case for the reopening of the Snow Hill tunnel between Farringdon and Blackfriars. The project came to fruition in 1988. Today, we have Thameslink, operating from Bedford and Luton, through central London and on to destinations such as Gatwick Airport and Brighton.

Linking together of two separate railways has its own problems, not least the level of traffic already in existence south of the Thames. Today's Thameslink is constrained unduly by capacity limitations in general

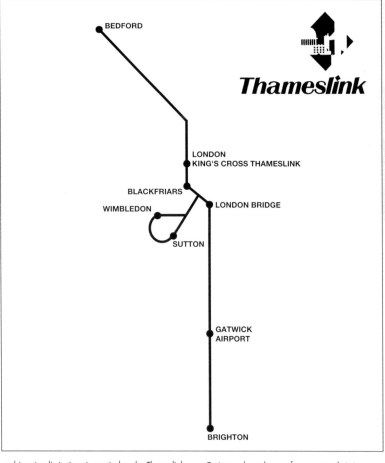

and junction limitations in particular; the Thameslink 2000 scheme hopes in due course to overcome these. What does Thameslink presently offer?

The single most serious limitation at present is the inability to find train paths through London Bridge in the peak, involving as it does access from Blackfriars and then crossing to the Brighton lines on the flat in the London Bridge area. The alternatives for trains from the Midland, both of which are used, are either:

- to divert to, and terminate at, Moorgate, or
- to run via Tulse Hill and reach the Brighton line at Streatham Common.

Trains southwards can of course start their journeys at London Bridge.

The peak service at present thus bears only a limited relationship to that at other times. During the day, Thameslink offers 8tph, four of which run throughout from Bedford via London Bridge to East Croydon, Gatwick Airport and Brighton. Of the remaining four:

- 1tph runs Luton to Sutton, via Wimbledon;
- 1tph runs St Albans to Sutton, via Wimbledon;
- 1tph runs Bedford to Sutton, direct; and
- 1tph runs Luton to Sutton, direct.

Above: In the new Thameslink livery, Class 319/0 unit No 319032 approaches Gatwick Airport station on 6 December 1994, forming the 1426 Three Bridges–Bedford service. *Brian Morrison*

All of the trains approaching Sutton continue on the loop back by the 'other' route, to Blackfriars and beyond. The services shown have a variety of stopping patterns, with trains from Bedford making only one intermediate call between St Albans and King's Cross Thameslink. One of these trains runs non-stop from Luton to King's Cross Thameslink, 30.50 miles in 28min.

Thameslink runs 5.7 million train miles a year, average journey 18 miles. This is worth £2.60 in revenue, and the passenger occupation rate at 80 passenger miles per train mile is close to the national average.

Operationally, Thameslink uses Class 319/0 and 319/1 dual-voltage units, the former without first class accommodation and the latter with. This does make stock working more difficult, and while the Brighton trains might be expected to have first class accommodation, the timetable shows that some do not. This would seem to make first class travel something of a lottery, even assuming that units do not stray from their booked workings. All units are maintained at Selhurst, which is also the home for the Class 319/0 units leased by Network SouthCentral.

In Charter terms, service reliability was 98.4% for 1994/95 (99.0% target) and punctuality was 91.4% against a target of 89.0%.

Thameslink 2000 plans also envisage the feeding in of Great Northern services from stations to Peterborough and to King's Lynn, while in the south services will be projected as now, plus East Grinstead, Eastbourne, Littlehampton, Bognor Regis and Guildford. The maximum throughput of the T2000 central section through City Thameslink is put at 24tph.

However, plans have changed before and they will doubtless change again. What effect will the Channel Tunnel Rail Link have, and will there be any through running from the CTRL on to the Midland or Thameslink?

West Anglia Great Northern Railway Ltd

The West Anglia Great Northern (WAGN) is a combination of the less glamorous side of Liverpool Street's operations and the more limited suburban operation on the GN out of King's Cross and also Moorgate. Unlike the situation south of the Thames, the use of three London termini is not accompanied by extensive inter-connections between the lines approaching them.

Services mostly operate on a half-hourly frequency, thus:

From Liverpool Street

● Enfield Town
● Cheshunt via Seven Sisters
● Chingford (3tph)

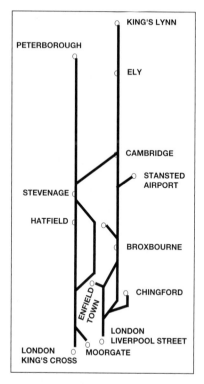

R A I L W A Y

Right: The underground section from Drayton Park to Moorgate is among the less prepossessing. An up train for Moorgate of unit No 313048 arrives at Old Street. *John Glover*

Below right: That King's Lynn should find itself as the terminus of an electrified railway from London must surely rank as a major political achievement. The alternative of a diesel unit connection to and from Cambridge would surely have been much less attractive. On 19 September 1992, unit No 317346 has just arrived with the 08.45 from King's Cross. *John Glover*

- Hertford East via Lea Valley
- principal stations to Bishop's Stortford via Lea Valley, with 1tph extended to Cambridge
- Stansted Airport, calling at Tottenham Hale and, alternate trains only, also at Bishop's Stortford

From Moorgate

- Welwyn Garden City
- Hertford North, with 1tph extended to Letchworth

From King's Cross

- Cambridge, non-stop (1tph)
- Cambridge, non-stop and stations to King's Lynn (1tph)
- Finsbury Park, Stevenage and Huntingdon (1tph)

- principal stations to Hitchin, extended alternately all stations to Peterborough or Cambridge

WAGN's outer-suburban services in particular are tightly timed. Pride of place must go to the King's Cross to Cambridge services, which cover the 58 miles in 52min, but King's Lynn and Huntingdon both have services timed at an average 60mph. This has benefits for the operators as well as passengers, since stock and staff can be that much better utilised.

The Stansted SkyTrain takes 41 or 42min for the 37.50 miles from Liverpool Street to Stansted Airport.

Inevitably, inner services have a less sparkling performance. For instance, to travel the 10.75 miles from Liverpool Street to Enfield Town, calling at all 14 stations, takes 30min. Moorgate to Enfield Chase takes 3min less. This points, perhaps, to the economics of inner-suburban operations compared with the longer distance journeys. Asset utilisation is poorer, costs increase due to the greater number of stations which need to be maintained and, probably, staffed as well, while revenue yield per passenger is relatively modest. Of course, if there are lots of passengers…

With annual train miles at 9.7 million, WAGN actually exceeds InterCity East Coast. But there the comparisons stop; WAGN's passengers travel no more than an average 16 miles and spend £2.38 in the process. Average train occupancy at 75 is similar to operations such as Thames Trains or Thameslink Rail.

The whole of the operation is electrified at 25kv ac, including the 99.25 miles out to King's Lynn, apart from the third unit section from Drayton Park to Moorgate. All operation is in the hands of multiple-units based at Hornsey. This comprises the whole of Class 317 for the outer suburban services and parts of Classes 313/315 for the inner operations. There

94

are also the five Class 322 Stansted Express units, based at Ilford, while use of the Class 365 Networker Express units is in prospect.

In performance terms, service reliability for Great Northern was 98.3% for 1994/95 (target 99.0%) and punctuality was 89.5% against a target of 91.0%. On the West Anglia side, reliability was 99.0% (target 98.5%) and punctuality was 92.6% against the same target of 91.0%.

The WAGN Railway faces substantial change in the medium to longer term. This is as a result of measures as diverse as:

- the traffic which might be generated by the Channel Tunnel Rail Link at St Pancras;
- the construction of Thameslink 2000, into which some (but only some) of the GN trains could be diverted; and
- the growth in the use of Stansted Airport.

The general view seems to be that WAGN has a relatively stable market, which expanded in the last decade following the King's Lynn electrification and that of the ECML to Peterborough. High commuting growth is likely to return once the recession ends.

Above: Loadhaul livery Class 56 No 56006 Ferrybridge 'C 'Power Station passes Ferrybridge on 4 October 1995 with an incoming train of MGR coal. *Brian Morrison*

The Freight Companies

Rail freight is not what it once was. In 1994/95, the total tonnes forwarded fell below 100 million. Compare that with the early days of British Railways when, in 1948, traffic levels were nearly three times greater. The commodity mix looked like this:

Table 8.1: Freight Train Traffic Originating, 1948			
	000 tons	%	av length of haul, miles
Merchandise	54,780	19.8	117
minerals (bricks, iron ore, limestone, pig iron, roadstone)	59,280	21.5	76
Coal and coke	161,145	58.4	55
Livestock	912	0.3	na
Total	276,117	100.0	72

For those who wonder about the tonnage of livestock, the Report conscientiously informed the reader that the tonnage equivalent of the number of horses, cattle, sheep, pigs etc was computed on a standard (but unspecified) basis.

But, even when converted into volumes as expressed in ton miles, the average length of rail haul in 1948 at 72 miles was only a little shorter than that of the 83 miles today. Meanwhile, road freight has expanded tremendously, now exceeding rail tonne mile volumes by a factor of 10.

Industrial changes are at least partly to blame, notably the significant restructuring in the traditional core businesses of coal and steel. Rail's past dependence on these areas is illustrated by the 1948 results.

Having shed the Speedlink wagon load business in 1991, the Board's freight activity was managed through two separate organisations. Trainload Freight, itself subdivided into the four profit centres of Coal, Metals, Construction and Petroleum, dealt essentially with bulk loads from private siding to private siding traffic.

Trainload Freight traffic in recent years has reflected the impact of recession in some industries and of energy policy in others. Power station coal, of which 60 million tonnes a year was carried as recently as 1991/92, is now expected to be no more than 35 million tonnes in the next couple of years. In the other main commodity areas, steel is expected to be around 15 million tonnes, aggregates 15 million tonnes also, and petroleum 10 million tonnes.

Bulk freight flows on rail should ideally meet the following specifications:

● volumes should be significant, typically above 100,000 tonnes a year;

● trains should run from source to destination with no intermediate marshalling;
● loading and unloading should take place at fixed origin and destination points;
● movements should be regular, ie daily or even several times a day; and
● full use should be made of locomotive power to maximise the train's carrying capacity.

Trainload Freight customers include National Power, British Steel, Amey Roadstone and Shell UK.

Below: Coal, the mainstay of the rail freight industry for so many years, has long been carried in large capacity merry-go-round hoppers. The 16-ton mineral wagons in the background of this picture taken at Guide Bridge in 1970 are now just a memory. *John Glover*

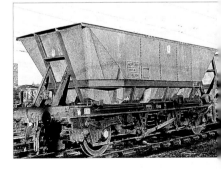

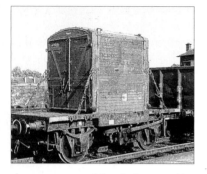

Their commitment, and that of others, to rail has included investing £1.5 billion in terminals and over £500 million in wagon fleets.

The other company, Railfreight Distribution, catered for longer distance general freight. Notably, this included containers, automotive traffic and international freight services.

Intermodal services operate in two distinct spheres. Deepsea is concentrated on the ports of Felixstowe, Southampton, Liverpool and Tilbury, and distributes over 400,000 deepsea port containers a year or around 35% of the market. The other is the UK/Irish business, centred on the Port of Liverpool, operating a road/rail combination which links into daily sailings to Ireland. Intermodal services are justified where trainload services are not justified or are physically impossible. Typically, road or ship will bring containers to terminals, where they are trunked to other terminals for distribution.

Compared with trainload, intermodal terminal handling operations represent an important element of the total movement and therefore of its cost. Also, they necessarily carry a time and reliability penalty. The combination of these factors suggests that a trunk movement of 200-250 miles is needed to overcome this competitive disadvantage.

To which may be added the Channel Tunnel, which greatly enlarges the directly served markets and the distances required to make intermodal a success. The Harwich train ferry closed in 1994, and the Dover facility in 1995. Through the tunnel, Manchester to Munich represents a 40hr rail journey, compared with 54hr by road over a distance of

Above: The 'A' container, in which no more than four tons could be carried, loaded on to a Conflat. *John Glover*

Below: The pick-up goods, here headed by a Gresley Class J6 0-6-0 No 64272 approaching Sutton Bridge with a train from Spalding on 30 July 1958. *G. S. Robinson*

Right: A pair of Class 87s with No 87035 leading pass Hest Bank with an up train of steel coil in August 1987. *John Glover*

Below right: Transrail livery is carried by Class 37/5 No 37673 as it backs into the driers adjacent to Burngullow Junction to pick up china clay wagons on 21 August 1995. Passing it is the 0740 Paddington–Penzance IC125 led by power car No 43151. *Brian Morrison*

(roundly) 980 miles. There are no hauls within Britain of that distance.

An initial five rail terminals in Britain are being expanded to around a dozen on present plans. The first continental destinations to be served directly included Madrid, Valencia, Milan, Vienna, Mannheim and Duisburg, with former Eastern Bloc countries and Rome to follow. RfD consider that there could eventually be 45 freight trains through the tunnel in each direction daily. This, however, would meet severe capacity problems in southeast England. Whether or not freight eventually uses the Channel Tunnel Rail Link, CTRL construction is the key to providing more overall line capacity in the Tunnel to the London corridor.

The restructuring of the BR freight businesses into a number of new companies at Government behest was intended 'to increase the opportunities for competition, lower entry barriers, and focus operations more closely on the needs of the customers and localities served'.

During 1994/95, the Trainload Freight business was split into three, broadly along geographical lines. The three companies are:

Above: Passing the unusual Snodland signalbox on 4 June 1995, Mainline-liveried Class 37/7 No 37803 hauls the 0033 engineers' train 6Z25 from Hoo Junction away from an overnight possession at Bat & Ball. *Brian Morrison*

- Loadhaul (based on TLF North East)
- Mainline Freight (TLF South East) and
- Transrail Freight (TLF West).

These companies also absorbed part of the domestic non-container business of Railfreight Distribution, as well as responsibility for provision of all rail services in support of BR Infrastructure Services (BRIS). Although based initially in defined areas, all of these businesses may operate anywhere in the country.

Loadhaul has the benefit of petroleum traffics from refineries on Humberside, Mainline Freight will have substantial aggregate traffics, while Transrail Freight has South Wales steel traffic. All, but Loadhaul especially, will share in power station coal movements; the location of the power station rather than the originating point of the coal determined the initial allocation between companies.

Each company had a 1994/95 turnover estimated at between £125 million and £150 million. The intention of the three-way split was to strike a balance between enhancing competition and retaining the economies of scale; of the 11,600 track miles which carried TLF traffic, more than half carry trains operated by more than one company and nearly a quarter by all three.

In terms of assets, each company owns its own light maintenance depots, plus a range of locomotive and wagon types. These do not belong to the leasing companies. Between 200 and 300 line locomotives, that is, excluding shunters, are owned by each. The wagon fleets as in 1992 were as follows:

Transrail introduced its less than trainload 'Enterprise' freight service in 1994. The basis is an overnight transit, initially on a Sittingbourne–Elgin route, with interchange at Warrington. Research had shown that there were many existing customers of 1,000 tonne trains who wished to send smaller consignments. This included previous users, if the price and the service could be got right. Also, the rail share of the consumer goods market was very low, and a viable and attractive alternative for palletised goods for break bulk distribution was possible. New intermodal equipment was compatible with 'Enterprise' trains, which could take ISO containers, trailertrain, etc. All these vehicles have the same riding characteristics.

Table 8.2: Locomotive and wagon fleets by freight sector, July 1992				
Sector	Locomotives		Wagons (traffic vehicles only)	
	Main Line	Shunters	BR owned	Privately owned
TLF Coal	220	42	9987	200
TLF Construction	76		236	2000
TLF Metals	95	107	3610	500
TLF Petroleum	79		6	6750
RfD Contract services	)	)	1268	)
RfD Other	)254	)226	42	)4000
Freightliner	)	)	1336	)
RES	109		796	-
Totals	833	375	17281	13450

It may be noted that the BR-owned wagon fleet was recorded as having reduced to 13,379 as at 31 March 1995. The comparison with the 1,165,166 wagons, albeit of rather less individual carrying capacity, which it took to move the traffics of 1948 referred to earlier, is remarkable.

The TLF successor company fleets also include locomotives and wagons for what used to be known as internal user traffic for maintaining the railway. Transrail, for instance, has a fleet of 3,500 such wagons. The company 'delivers a logistics service, which includes resourcing and managing train operation, hauling materials from source to destination and transporting spoil and waste materials in specialist rolling stock dedicated to your contract'. Also available are long-welded rail and cable-laying trains, and track inspection trains. Transrail also handle the BR Telecommunications contract. BRT has its own fleet of Bescot-based Class 20 locomotives and wagons. These are maintained by Transrail, who also undertake the planning and control of all BRT train movements throughout the country.

The outlook is for a 'hub and spoke' facility, but with road collection to and from Railfreight terminals. Specimen timings are Sittingbourne 1200, London 1600, Bescot 1900, Warrington 2100–2300, Mossend 0400 and Elgin 1200. This links with a St Blazey–Teesside service at Warrington. The object is to make the best use of existing resources in providing an overnight everywhere-to-everywhere service in Britain, to which Warrington would be the key.

Later, the 'Enterprise' service is also to cover Wakefield, Merseyside, Blackburn, Washwood Heath, Stratford and others. North Wales is to be brought in by use of Departmental services to Penmaenmawr. Resources are not tied to any particular area or traffic type. However, main line locomotives are just too expensive to be deployed for low traffic levels, and the train locomotive is used to pick up and set down traffic at terminals *en route* as the train passed. In itself, a Class 08 costs only c£20k per annum, but this rises to six figures if it is manned round the clock.

Trains of 1,500–2,000 tonnes are a possibility, to brinf the unit haulage costs down.

It is now 30 years since Freightliner services were introduced between London (York Way) and Glasgow (Gushetfaulds). The company has been separated from Railfreight Distribution as Freightliner (1995) Ltd, for transfer to the private sector. Freightliner operates 13 terminals, but suffers from high unit costs. RfD continues to be responsible for the international intermodal and automotive freight businesses.

Rail Express Systems' principal customer is the Royal Mail, which accounts for 70% of the company's business. A new distribution hub has been completed at Willesden and is the key to a long-term contract between RES and the Post Office for the carriage of mail by rail. The contract is based on an entirely new train plan based on three waves of mail trains, one in the afternoon, one in the early evening and the final one late at night. At the same time, Royal Mail withdrew from all its London passenger terminal operations to concentrate on the Willesden hub adjacent to the North Circular Road. This combines Royal Mail's London distribution centre and a seven-platform station. Trains depart from here for Scotland, the West Country, South Wales, Kent, the

Above: Class 31 locomotives Nos 31554 and 31533 pass Droitwich Spa with a southbound permanent way train on 24 March 1992. *John Glover*

North West, the North East and East Anglia. Further railhubs are being constructed at Doncaster and Warrington.

The contract lasts until 2006. For this, the fleet of 16 four-car Class 325 Parcel Units has been built by ABB Derby. These are owned by Royal Mail, with operation and maintenance contracted to RES. The Class 325s have roller shutter doors and are based on the Class 319 Thameslink vehicles. The Class 325s thus have dual ac/dc capabilities, but are also designed to be hauled by diesel traction when their duties take them away from the electrified network. Alternatively, containers of mail (not mailbags!) will be loaded into Super GUVs (General Utility Vans) with roller shutter doors and new floors. These are hauled vehicles, using ex-Class 307 Driving Trailers at Propelling Control Vehicles (PCVs) in a push-pull formation.

RES also has a contract to move locomotives and stock to and from repair points on behalf of the rolling stock leasing companies, since it has the unique asset among the operating companies of a track access agreement with Railtrack which covers the whole of the network. This reflects its role as essentially a network business.

Consequently, RES is also the provider of non-timetabled operations such as private charters and the movement of the Royal Train. It is also the only operator with a safety case to operate steam train services.

There are also likely to be new entrants to the railway industry. Both Foster-Yeoman Ltd and ARC Ltd as the constituent companies of Mendip Rail have a small fleet of Class 59 heavy-haul locomotives from General Motors, to which must now be added National Power. While these fleets have been acquired for stated specific purposes, there is no reason to assume that these companies and indeed others will not seek to expand. Thus British Nuclear Fuels have acquired some Class 20s for nuclear flask traffic from Sellafield, through their subsidiary Direct Rail Services. This traffic was previously conveyed by Transrail.

New operators on the railway will have to:

● satisfy Railtrack's safety validation;
● obtain a licence from the Rail Regulator; and
● negotiate an access agreement with Railtrack.

Access agreements of course have to be entered into by all freight operators, although agreements made for previously existing traffics are not subject to the approval of the Regulator. Normally, the Regulator will need to be satisfied that the proposed agreements are not framed in such a way that they represent the abuse of a monopoly position, create undue discrimination between users of a facility, or unduly limit competition in the provision of railway services. Nor must the agreements be woolly; rights and obligations will need to be clearly specified and also scrutinised to check that they are legally robust.

However, there is also the matter of the charges to be made by Railtrack. Here, the Rail Regulator has published a policy statement.

Given that it is still early days and much is still to be learned, the Regulator intends to apply the following criteria:

● charges should be greater than or equal to the avoidable costs incurred by Railtrack as a direct result of carrying that particular freight flow;
● charges should be less than or equal to the standalone cost which would be incurred by a notional efficient operator;
● charges should not be higher or lower, after

Above: Freightliner was the 1960s answer to rail freight's problems. *Author's collection*

allowing for specific factors relevant to each case, than those for other operators or users to such an extent that they risk significantly distorting competition between rail freight operators or users; and
● the structure of charges should broadly reflect the value to users of access to the rail network, and should enable Railtrack to recover its total freight-specific costs plus any expected contribution to the shared common costs of its passenger and freight services.

In short, the aim is to stop Railtrack making charges which are excessive, which distort competition between freight operators, or which result in cross-subsidies. These last might be between individual freight users, or between freight and passenger services.

The Regulator's success, or otherwise, in achieving his objectives will become clearer as time progresses.

Another matter for consideration of those in the freight business is the potential of some financial help from the Government in the form of:
● an expanded freight facilities grants scheme,

Above: Freightliner relied traditionally on large gantry cranes spanning the tracks. Was a cheaper alternative a possibility? This picture from the 1989 Railfreight exhibition at Cricklewood shows what can be achieved. *John Glover*

Above right: A 'Bell-liner' from Willesden Euroterminal to Dollands Moor yard and mainland Europe passes Bickley Junction on 25 March 1995 powered by RfD Class 47/3 No 47.326 *Saltley Depot Quality Assured. Brian Morrison*

Right: The Class 59s are all owned by newcomers to the scene. Class 59/1 No 59104 *Village of Great Elm* passes Sidcup on 16 October 1995 with the 0958 6V17 Allington-Southall yard aggregates. This is an ARC Ltd-owned machine. *Brian Morrison*

which may provide Government grants for capital expenditure on railway facilities. This now includes all railway equipment, including locomotives, and takes account of reductions in rail traffic on motorways and inter-urban dual-carriageway roads (s139, Railways Act 1993). The eligible road mileage saved is valued at 5p per mile.

● a grant of up to 100% to contribute towards track access charges levied by Railtrack, where the traffic would otherwise move by road and there are environmental or other wider benefits to be gained (s137).

A total allocation of £43m over the three years until 31 March 1997 has been made for these two schemes combined. By comparison, grants under the previous scheme (s8, Railways Act 1974) were running at £2m-£3m a year.

A further encouragement to freight on rail is the Government decision to allow HGVs which carry goods in containers or swap-bodies to and from railheads to operate at a maximum 44 tonnes gross weight. The purpose is to encourage combined transport operations; it does not include the Eurotunnel shuttle services or ports. Vehicle drivers must carry documentation that their consignments are carried both by rail and by road to confirm the status of the goods being carried.

The whole of the railway freight operations are destined for the private sector; the interest of Wisconsin Central of Illinois in the former TLF portfolio, owners of RES, and a leading member of the consortium which owns New Zealand Rail Ltd was widely anticipated. At the beginning of 1996, it transpired that industry's unease on the advisability of the three-way split was reflected in political

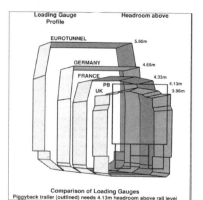

Above: Comparison of loading gauges. The piggyback trailer, outlined, needs 4.13m headroom above rail level. *The Piggyback Consortium.*

Below: New Class 325 emus for the Post Office Nos 325007/06/05 were to be found in line at ABB Works at Derby on 7 July 1995. *Brian Morrison*

action; the Transport Secretary announced that the three Trainload companies would be merged back into one company and sold as such to one of two American bidders. The enemy of rail freight in Britain is not other rail companies, but the road freight businesses.

Besides the Channel Tunnel and the CTRL link, where are the other new opportunities? Domestic waste is a growing market for rail as the easier nearby sites are exhausted, but what about piggyback technology?

Piggyback means carrying road trailers on rail wagons, without tractor units or their drivers. It is common in North America, where flat wagons can be used, and is also found in Continental Europe. However, bridges and tunnels are lower in Europe and special 'pocket' wagons with a wide space between the frames have been used. Cranes pick up the trailer and place it on the wagon so that the wheels drop into the 'pocket', where the tyres are only 330mm above the running rails. Could the limitations of the even more restrictive width and height of the British loading gauge be overcome?

The Piggyback Consortium think that it can. This group of 37 freight transport operators, port and terminal operators, rail track authorities, local authorities and others are dedicated to studying the feasibility of piggybacking 4 million high road semi-trailers through Britain on specially designed wagons. An initial study concluded that:

- rolling stock could be built to carry the semi-trailers past British platforms;
- the cost of upgrading the spine route from the Channel Tunnel to Ireland/Scotland via the WCML and Holyhead/Heysham/Stranraer was about £70m; and
- there is a worthwhile market for piggyback.

A detailed feasibility study is planned by the Consortium and Railtrack, and there is a prototype wagon.

Finally, the Royal Commission on Environmental Pollution report of October 1994 called for rail's freight market share to rise from 7% to 20% by 2010, which broadly means restoring the 1948 position with which this chapter began. How might this be achieved, and to what extent is technology the answer? To raise freight volumes by a third would undoubtedly be a hard task, but we cannot say that 'it can't be done!'

Rolling Stock Companies

The three rolling stock companies (ROSCOs) are Angel Train Contracts Ltd, Eversholt Leasing Ltd and Porterbrook Leasing Co Ltd. Together, they own about 11,000 passenger vehicles and locomotives which are leased to the Train Operating Companies. The leasing system means that capital costs are no longer a factor to be contended with by the TOCs; they get what they pay for on a long-term contract. Whether this is precisely what they want, at the price which they judge they can afford, is perhaps another matter.

For the time being, anyway, only home-grown rolling stock is suitable for use within the restrictive British loading gauge, while any new stock added to the overall fleet is likely only to result in the withdrawal of locomotives and units built in the 1960s or even earlier. Fleet shortages do not, of course, manifest themselves uniformly across all rolling stock types, while there are also new technical requirements to be met. Fire safety regulations will severely restrict what can (or cannot) work into Heathrow Airport when the infrastructure work there is completed, while opportunities for through workings which link Clapham Junction and the south with Willesden Junction and the north will put a premium on dual voltage emus. Similarly, the advent of the Robin Hood and Ivanhoe lines, together with expansion in Strathclyde, increase the requirement for diesel units. As matters stand, a few Modernisation Plan vehicles are still in service, with no replacements in sight. And then, on InterCity services, the IC125s will not last for ever...

Such problems are for the leasing companies, perhaps in conjunction with the rolling stock manufacturers, to sort out. It is also the ROSCOs' responsibility to finance their businesses and pay for such heavy maintenance as may be required. The TOCs are not, however, bound to obtain any extra rolling stock that they might need from the ROSCOs, if they can find another source.

Each Train Operating Company has entered into a Master Lease with one or more ROSCOs. These contain the basic lease conditions, as opposed to the detailed ones for each fleet concerning the rentals and a lease length of up to 10 years.

The following are some of the obligations of the TOC:

- payment of rent to the ROSCO;
- carrying out running repairs and maintenance;
- use the rolling stock only in accordance with its permitted use
- securing and paying for third party insurance;
- fault rectification; and
- return of rolling stock at the end of the lease in the condition specified.

The corresponding obligations of the ROSCO are:
- supply of the rolling stock in an agreed condition;
- allowing the TOC to use the stock without let or hindrance;
- procurement of heavy maintenance and repairs;
- paying for any mandatory modifications; and
- securing property damage insurance, which is recharged to the TOC.

HM Railway Inspectorate

The Inspectorate is now part of the Health & Safety Executive. The Railway Inspectorate's objectives are to ensure the continued safety of Britain's railways by the following means:

The issue of guidance for railway operations on the design, construction and operation of railways

The 'Railway Safety Principles and Guidance' is being republished from 1996 in two parts. Part 1 sets out the principles and gives an indication of the factors to be taken into account in implementation. Part 2 consists of eight separate sections dealing with specific aspects of railway construction and gives examples of good practice. These sections are:

A	The Infrastructure
B	Stations
C	Electric Traction Systems
D	Signalling
E	Level Crossings
F	Trains
G	Tramways
H	Heritage Railways

Three plus two seating each side of a gangway has in many cases been an economic necessity. These three photographs show some past attempts at making the arrangement acceptable. They are:

Above: Interior of a Class 303 Scottish 'Blue Train', 1959.

Left: Interior of a 4SUB unit, Southern Region, c1948.

Below: Interior of Class 210 experimental demu, 1981.

What new ideas will the rolling stock companies offer? *John Glover (3)*

Above: A fixed red colour light at Lichfield City, photographed on 20 February 1993, prevents trains from proceeding towards Trent Valley, but the subsidiary signals allow entry to the sidings.
John Glover

Prior inspection and approval of new lines, rolling stock and equipment

Proposals are considered by the Inspectorate. New infrastructure can range from minor platform lengthening or track layout revisions to the construction of Ashford International station, Sheffield Supertram or the Channel Tunnel Rail Link. The Inspectorate gives type approval to new locomotives and rolling stock, including track maintenance machines.

The monitoring of safety procedures on existing lines, to ensure compliance with the Health and Safety at Work Act and relevant statutory provisions

The Inspectorate has powers to investigate any notifiable accident or dangerous occurrence, inspect premises or issue notices in respect of potentially dangerous procedures or breaches of legislation.

The investigation of selected accidents, and the study of accident trends to identify priorities for improvement

The Inspectorate has investigated accidents from 1842, although it did not have the formal powers so to do until the Regulation of Railways Act 1871. It issues reports and makes many recommendations. An Annual Report is issued, containing many statistics and accident records.

These are perhaps the traditional areas of interest of HMRI within a unified railway. The job is changing and the following principles (abridged) have been agreed as fundamental for railway safety:

● Any system must not lead to any diminution of current safety standards, should be practical and able to deliver appropriate and effective control of risk;

● the prime responsibility of ensuring safety must rest with the party who has control, to the extent that they actually have that control;

● the degree of statutory control shall be the minimum consistent with the need to ensure adequate and cost-effective levels of control of risk and to secure public confidence;

● any arrangements should be demonstrably fair to all parties involved; and

● legislation pertaining to railway safety should be administered by a single independent safety regulator, the HSE.

From these, other principles have been derived:

● safety systems on the railway must address technical, operational and organisational issues;

● duties and responsibilities must be adequately defined;

● within the limits of their control, the infrastructure controllers will bear primary responsibility for the co-ordination of measures to control risk on the railway; and

● there must be effective co-ordination and co-operation between all parties and individuals.

This is not a treatise on railway safety, which is a subject in its own right. Suffice to say here that all operators have to submit a railway safety case (RSC). This demonstrates that an operator has the systems in place to manage operations safely and meet required safety standards. It includes a safety policy, a risk assessment, a description of safety management systems, and the safety side of maintenance and operational arrangements.

The RSCs of train and station operators must be

Above: Overhead clearances need to be monitored. This method, simple but effective, is installed here at the exit from Bletchley Traction Maintenance Depot. The bells will ring if touched by a high vehicle; they are commonly installed at farm crossings.
John Glover

validated and accepted by Railtrack, which also regularly monitors them. Railtrack's own RSC must be validated and accepted by HMRI, who also view other operators' safety cases to ensure that they are properly considered by Railtrack.

HMRI is also concerned with the standards of competence for safety-critical staff, and is responsible for enforcement.

ASSOCIATION *of* TRAIN OPERATING COMPANIES

Association of Train Operating Companies

The Association of Train Operating Companies (ATOC) has been set up as an unincorporated association by its members to administer essential inter-operator commercial activities and become the trade association of the passenger rail industry. All 25 TOCs are members, as are European Passenger Services.

ATOC's principal objectives are to facilitate the development and operation of commercial arrangements between passenger operators and to promote the use of the railway network (including, in particular, the making of journeys which involve the services of more than one operator). The agreements have been put in place for the following reasons:

- to enable participants to offer network-wide products to passengers;
- to fulfil licence or franchise conditions imposed to safeguard passenger interests; and
- to perpetuate elements of the BR organisation which would otherwise be under threat with the disaggregation of the passenger rail industry.

The ATOC schemes cover a number of areas:

- The offering by passenger operators individually and collectively of new and existing fare types, Discount Cards and reservations and, in addition, goods and services provided by third parties, including travel on London Transport services. Fares may be for travel only on the trains of a single passenger operator or may be inter-available and/or through fares.

- The honouring of fares, Discount Cards and reservations by carriers and the carriage of passengers subject to the national conditions of carriage.

- The retailing of these products by passenger operators and third parties, including travel agents and providers of other means of transport.

- The provision of passenger information through the operation of Telephone Enquiry Bureaux.

- The provision of staff travel facilities, comprising reciprocal rights between the passenger operators themselves and with certain third parties as well as non-reciprocal rights with some third parties.

- The allocation of revenues between passenger-carrying operators and the payment of commission to both retailing passenger operators and third parties.

- The settlement of sums due between passenger operators and to and from some third parties through the mechanism of the Railway Settlement Plan.

ATOC is also involved with other key players in the passenger rail industry, including the Department of Transport, the British Railways Board, major suppliers such as Railtrack, the rolling stock leasing companies, and the Passenger Transport Executives. ATOC is funded by members' subscriptions, scheme participation fees and from specially commissioned work for members.

Above: A variety of emus at the south end of London Bridge on 3 November 1994. From left to right, these are Class 456 units Nos 456003 on the 1048 to East Croydon and 456004 on ecs to depot, Class 319/0 No 319019 on the 1033 to Sutton, and Class 465016 at the rear of the 0947 Gravesend-Charing Cross via Bexleyheath. ATOC will help sort out disputes between companies.
Brian Morrison

European Passenger Services

European Passenger Services (EPS) is the British company running Eurostar, a service provided jointly by the railways of Belgium, Britain and France. EPS was set up by the British Railways Board. In April 1994, ownership was vested in the UK Government.

Services commenced on 14 November 1994 between the five-platformed Waterloo International and Paris Nord or Brussels Midi, with a journey time of 3hr to Paris (308 miles) and 3hr 15min to Brussels (237 miles). Service levels since have been increased progressively, with 11 weekday trains in each direction to Paris and six to Brussels by early 1996. Service provision is marginally less on Sundays. Intermediate calls are made, on a limited number of services, at the privately funded and built Ashford International, Calais Fréthun and Lille. It is anticipated that full operation will see two international trains leaving London every hour.

Onward TGV connections are available directly from Lille, while Brussels provides connections to Amsterdam, Frankfurt and Berlin. At home, IC125s running under contract to EPS provide services from Waterloo to both the East and West Coast main lines, while the GW TOC and RR SW&W both operate between Waterloo and the West of England/South Wales.

Services are provided by 31 Eurostar sets of Class 373 stock at a cost of around £20 million each, divided into 11 UK-owned, 16 French and 4 Belgian. An operational train set consists of two identical nine-coach half sets and a power car on each end. Sets are articulated within themselves. Trains contain 210 first class seats and 584 second class seats (total 794) and are 393.48m long. First class accommodation thus accounts for 26.5% of the total.

The follow-on order for seven shorter north of London trains of seven-coach half sets commence

111

Above: Waterloo International at platform level, before the station opened. *John Glover*

operation in 1996 from Edinburgh (ECML), Manchester (WCML) and Birmingham (WCML) to Paris and Brussels on cyclic diagrams. These services will displace the IC125s to and from those destinations.

All Eurostar sets are maintained at North Pole International, reached via the West London Line.

Separately, European Night Services (ENS) purchased 72 sleepers, 47 reclining seat coaches and 20 service vehicles; a total of 139 for the night services. ENS has been formed by EPS, which has the majority 61.5% shareholding (and hence 85 of the 139 coaches), Dutch (NS) and German (DB) Railways 13.5% each and SNCF 11.5%. SNCB has an option to take up a share in the future.

This investment is for the overnight sleeper services between London and Amsterdam and Frankfurt/Dortmund. There will also be sleepers from South Wales and from Glasgow via the WCML to Paris and Brussels. Additional requirements are for 7 Class 92 locomotives, 12 Class 37s, and two Class 73s and a Class 08 for shunting and rescue duties. Also acquired are five generator cars, converted former Mk3 sleepers.

The bill for the station at Waterloo International was £130 million, with North Pole International Depot at £85 million. The private sector Ashford International station builders, John Laing plc, will be remunerated by a toll from each of the annual 2 million or so passengers using it, payable by the international train service operators and probably around £1 per head.

LONDON ~ CONTINENTAL

London-Continental

Together with Union Railways, EPS was transferred to London & Continental Railways in summer 1996. L&C were the successful company in the competition to build and operate the Channel Tunnel Rail Link. Eurostar services are thus helping to provide a revenue stream which will help fund the construction of the CTRL. Effectively, this will create a vertically-integrated operation, in contrast to the domestic scene of Railtrack, Train Operating Company and ROSCO.

un␣ion

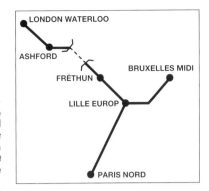

Union Railways

Union Railways Ltd was created in 1992 as a wholly-owned BR agency company to plan and design the proposed high speed rail link between London and the Channel Tunnel. In March 1993, the Government announced their choice of a northern route to an expanded St Pancras station and that the project would be developed as a joint venture between the public and private sectors.

The 109km (68-mile) route is designed to provide additional line capacity, reduce journey times and to promote economic regeneration of the East Thames corridor. An intermediate station, for both international and domestic traffics, is now in place at Ashford, which requires a small diversion from the

Right: Waterloo International, with passengers joining trains. *John Glover*

Below: UK Eurostar set No 3013 approaches Vauxhall with the 0753 Waterloo–Paris Nord on 23 November 1995. *John Glover*

CTRL main line. Other stations, again international and domestic, will be built at Ebbsfleet, and Stratford.

Junctions with the existing railway, besides those at Ashford, will be made south of Ebbsfleet where a link to Swanley and Waterloo would be engineered, and at Ebbsfleet itself with a junction from the North Kent line, Northfleet and Gravesend. Freight traffic would leave the CTRL at Ripple Lane, while onward connecting lines would be available in the immediate area of St Pancras. For rolling stock purposes, a London-facing junction would be provided at Stratford to allow access to a new servicing and maintenance facility on the Temple Mills yard site.

Speeds of up to 185mph are envisaged, but provision will be made for freight. The CTRL is considered capable of reducing the London to Paris or Brussels journey time by half an hour, while Ashford might gain commuter trains to London taking 40min to St Pancras instead of the present 75min to a London terminus. Similar journey time reductions would be achieved from Folkestone and Canterbury West and, to a lesser extent, from the Medway towns eastwards.

The Channel Tunnel Rail Link Bill is presently before Parliament.

There are, of course, many other organisations whose businesses depend largely on the railway industry. Some, such as the former British Rail Engineering Ltd, have been in the private sector for several years. Others, such as Business Systems or BR Telecoms are now in the course of making the change; while a third group includes firms such as Pandrol Rail Fastenings Ltd, which have never been in the public sector.

Space considerations have dictated that only the major players can be discussed here, but the omission of the rest does not in any way seek to minimise their contribution.

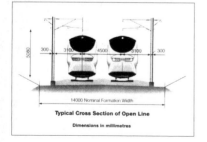

Above & below: Eurostar trains and some possible infrastructure layouts which will be used in the Channel Tunnel Rail Link. *Union Railways*

Above: Well, it is a nice poster, but is a disused garage forecourt in Woolwich really the best place to display it?
John Glover

Above right: St Pancras today is sadly underused. With all the Bedford local services now diverted south of the river or to Moorgate, there are seldom more than two trains in the station at once. In July 1977, No 45126 leaves with an early evening express to Sheffield, showing some of the available space which will be utilised to terminate Eurostar services. These trains are the length equivalent of 19 conventional coaches.
John Glover

Right: St Pancras façade. *John Glover*

Following pages: Map of Union Railways.

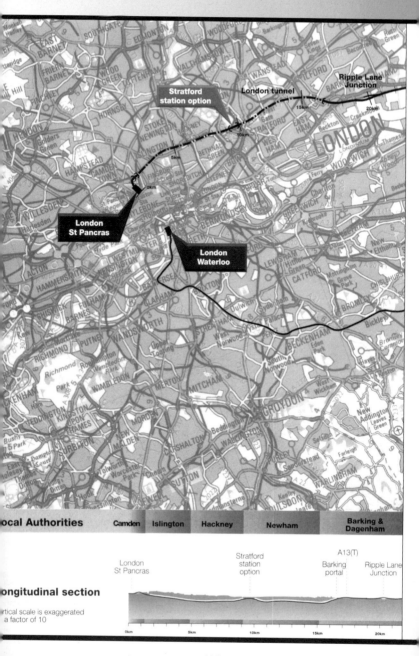

Stratford station option

London tunnel

Ripple Lane Junction

10km

5km

15km

20km

0km

LONDON

London St Pancras

London Waterloo

Local Authorities	Camden	Islington	Hackney	Newham	Barking & Dagenham

London St Pancras

Stratford station option

A13(T)

Barking portal

Ripple Lane Junction

Longitudinal section

Vertical scale is exaggerated by a factor of 10

0km   5km   10km   15km   20km

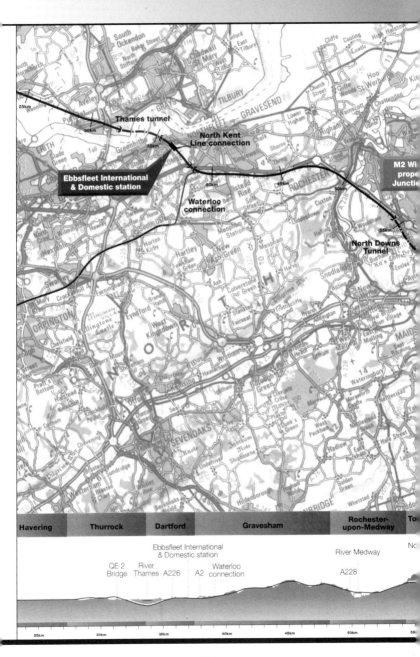

South Ockendon · North Stifford · Baker Street · Linford · East Tilbury

TILBURY · GRAYS · GRAVESEND · Cliffe · Cooling · High Halstow · Castle · Hoo St Werburgh

Thames tunnel

North Kent Line connection

Ebbsfleet International & Domestic station

M2 Wi propo Junctio

Waterloo connection

North Downs Tunnel

ROCHESTER

MAID

ORPINGTON

SEVENOAKS

25km · 30km · 35km · 40km · 45km · 48km · 50km · 55km

| Havering | Thurrock | Dartford | Gravesham | Rochester-upon-Medway | To |

Ebbsfleet International & Domestic station

River Medway

No

QE 2 Bridge · River Thames · A226 · A2 · Waterloo connection · A228

25km · 30km · 35km · 40km · 45km · 50km · 58

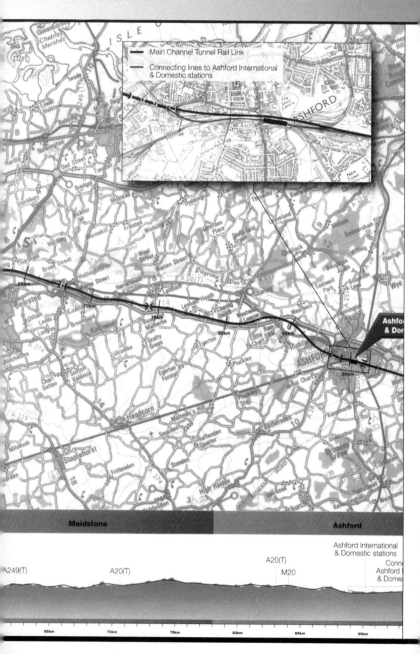

Main Channel Tunnel Rail Link

Connecting lines to Ashford International
& Domestic stations

ISLE

ASHFORD

Maidstone

Ashford

Ashford International
& Domestic stations

A249(T)

A20(T)

A20(T)
M20

Conn
Ashford
& Dome

65km   70km   75km   80km   85km   90km

Channel Tunnel

Ashford International
& Domestic stations

FOLKESTONE

HYTHE

ROMNEY

St Mary's Bay

Shepway

Based upon the current edition of the O
'Routemaster' series map and reproduced by t
with the sanction of H.M. Stationery Office.

ternational
tic stations

Connections to
Ashford International
& Domestic stations

A20(T)   A20(T)

95km   100km   105km

Above: A Networker set at the southeastern end of Waterloo East shows the Jubilee Line extension works for Southwark station in the foreground on 25 November 1995. A pedestrian connection to the Waterloo East platforms will be made in the area on the left-hand end of this picture. *John Glover*

Below: Down Anglia services on the GE main line have the Driving Brake Second Open (DBSO) at the leading end of the train. As it passes Stratford, the 0830 Liverpool Street–Norwich overhauls No 315804 as the latter returns to depot on 8 February 1990. *John Glover*

Making It All Work

Have the railways been managed inefficiently? The British Railways Board recorded the following in their Annual Report for 1994/95:

to decide what sort of railway they want to see in the future, and for the professionals to foster the debate and help them to achieve their political aims. But, for

Table 10.1: BR International Performance Indicators (1993/94 year)		
Comparison	British Rail Average	Other CER railways
Train kilometres per member of staff	3,463	2,220
Average passenger train loading (nos)	83	130
Average freight train loading (tonnes)	267	319
Support from public funds as % of GDP	0.18	0.59

In production terms, train kilometres per member of British Rail staff at 56% above the Community of European Railways (CER) average was decidedly commendable, but production of train km is of little value if they cannot be sold. Here, BR appeared much weaker; the average passenger train load on BR at 83 compared very unfavourably with the CER figure of 130. Freight was hardly more flattering at 267 tonne/km per train, compared with the CER's 319. On the other hand, in proportionate terms much less public finance went into the railways of Britain; perhaps, one might argue, you get what you pay for.

Crudely, it would seem that BR operations have been relatively efficient, but that the volume of passenger service provision in particular was over-generous for the traffic actually on offer.

Whatever the reasons, it is difficult to avoid the conclusion that 'we could do better'. What can the railway do most usefully and most successfully in the future, for the benefit of the nation as well as itself? This is not a question about matters of ownership or competition, which are relatively peripheral. Rather, it is addressing the long term aims of GB Ltd's overall strategy, and the political willingness or otherwise to dedicate the necessary level of resources. For, whilst railways may and perhaps should meet their operational costs through revenue from customers, the meeting of major investment costs can be all but impossible. There is a clear need for a statement of aims, to be supported by a general framework for decision making, and associated with both political and social vision.

Few would suggest that there is any place for the low quality, bargain basement railway in the 1990s and beyond. The industry can do much better than that. However, it is the prerogative of the politicians

progress to be made, there does need to be agreement on what the fundamental questions and issues really are.

The Problem Areas

What are the main transport problems facing Britain? According to the Department of Transport, these include:

- Overall passenger mileage by all modes, which is now running at three times 1951 levels, but is satisfied mostly by private cars.
- Growth of car ownership, from 14% of households in 1951 to 66% in 1989. At 374 cars per 1,000 population in 1990, this compared with 417 in France, 490 in the former West Germany and 648 in the USA.
- Forecasts of continued traffic growth, related to GDP, with demand in the range of 83% to 142% of 1988 levels by the year 2025.
- Growth of traffic congestion, which cannot be met by any conceivably acceptable road-building programme, least of all in cities.
- Growth in personal mobility, trade, resourcing of industry and retail distribution, with an increasing dominance of out-of-town locations for leisure and shopping activities.
- Environmental considerations, including noise, infrastructure impact, air pollution and global warming.

There is a limit to the contribution which even the most effective railway can make to such a range of problems, but a necessary precursor is to find a sensible form of railway organisation to meet the challenge. What does the railway presently achieve?

Table 10.2:	Market share by different passenger transport modes, 1994	
	Passenger km (billions)	% of total
British Rail	29	4
other railways	6	1
Buses and Coaches	43	6
Cars and Vans	596	87
Motor Cycles	4	1
Pedal Cycles	5	1
Air (domestic)	5	1
Total	689	100

Source: Transport Statistics 1995, Department of Transport

The extent of the eclipse of public transport modes is thus quite overwhelming; British Rail now accounts for a mere 4% of the total passenger miles, or little more than a quarter of the 15% achieved in 1952. Actual volumes of rail passengers have changed little; this is unlike the bus industry over the same period, which has declined remorselessly. The key change is in the growth of private road transport.

From these figures, various conclusions can be drawn:

● First, British Rail with 4% of the market can hardly be held to exercise general monopoly powers, whatever its future ownership. That said, rail is dominant in the Central London commuter business, while it is said to have up to 40% of some InterCity markets.

● Secondly, road traffic growth cannot continue to grow at the rate evident in the post-World War 2 years. This is not a political statement; merely it is a reflection on the infrastructure resources which would be needed to sustain that growth and the environmental consequences, in the widest sense, which would follow.

● Thirdly, it is evident both from its continued level of usage over the years and the general affection which rail holds in the public's eye that a smartly run, well promoted and modernised rail system is the principal contender to take a higher proportion of market share. The British people have always loved railways, but never the companies which run them.

It follows that, if the positive technical attributes of rail can be harnessed, exploited and developed, a new railway age might be at hand.

Rail is in all respects an integrated *system*, in which colossal numbers of potentially conflicting movements are being made all the time over large geographical areas. The actions of each train operator thus impinge directly on many others, a situation to which only the system controller can bring order. This affects both the planning stage and actual day-to-day operation. Unlike other modes of transport, the British Rail we knew had service provision, operational control and infrastructure engineering under a central body, albeit devolved latterly to a series of businesses. As recorded above, BR productivity compared well internationally with that of other administrations.

But, on its own, this is not enough. Like any other business, the railway needs to be oriented primarily towards the purchasers of its products, its customers. In the end, the present and the potential customers are more important than the operations managers and the engineers on whom the railway depends to make it all happen.

This is not, in any sense, to decry the contributions of the latter. Effective and efficient production methods, with quality control, are immensely important. The rail businesses, passenger and freight alike, cannot sell what they cannot deliver. The aim is to keep unit costs down, but also to explore and exploit technical advances.

There is no reason to doubt that private sector organisations could run the railways of Britain well; the concern is whether the Government's intended

method of proceeding will meet the needs of 21st century Britain and the European Community to which this country belongs, and the technical and operational requirements of a railway system.

Investment will be a major concern. Private and public finance will need to be used together for investment in railway rolling stock and infrastructure, and the right business environment must be created by the Government to make this happen.

Privatisation must assist and not hinder this process, and the railways need help and encouragement during this period of unprecedented change.

And the overall verdict? The jury will be out for some time yet. The Transport Correspondent of *The Times* summed the situation up rather neatly[1]:

'This privatisation is like no other attempted anywhere else on earth. It was a fudge between the competitive ideology of the Thatcherite right in the mid-1980s and the real-world practicalities of running a railway. The resulting structure is simultaneously clever and fiendishly complicated. By Christmas 1996, we will know whether it was the work of geniuses or madmen.'

Meanwhile, it is up to those in the rail transport industry to do everything in their power to make the new system work, for the mutual benefit of the railway businesses, their customers and their staff.

[1]Jonathan Prynn, *The Times*, 17 November 1995.

Above: In the yard at the new National Power depot at Ferrybridge are two newly-arrived Class 59/2 locomotives, Nos 59202/04. What other use might be made of such machines in the future? The date is 18 August 1995. *Brian Morrison*

Below: This is the cover from a Southern Region booklet distributed to commuters well over 30 years ago, in 1962. The gist of the contents was 'You may think you could do it better than we can, but have you any idea what is involved?' Well, for a start... *John Glover*

Below: Radio electronic tokenless block was installed on the East Suffolk line. The receiving aerial on the front of the Class 101 may be seen, as can the mast on the roof of Woodbridge station building. This Lowestoft–Ipswich service was photographed on 21 July 1988. *John Glover*

Appendix 1: Principal Acts of Parliament and European Legislation

Domestic legislation

The Acts listed, together with their major objectives, are those which directly affected the railways from Nationalisation onwards. The annual private acts promoted by the British Railways Board and its predecessors, mainly for the authorisation to carry out new works, are omitted.

1947   Transport Act
Nationalisation of the railways, London Transport, road haulage, docks and inland waterways. Creation of the British Transport Commission (BTC) with the Railway Executive as one of its subsidiaries.

1953   Transport Act
Disposal of the Road Haulage Executive; abolition of the Railway Executive.

1962   Transport Act
Abolition of the BTC and creation of the British Railways Board (BRB), and others. Deficit grants for BRB. A formalised passenger service closure procedure, with Ministerial decision after consideration by the Transport Users' Consultative Committee.

1968   Transport Act
Establishment of the National Freight Corporation, Passenger Transport Authorities and Executives, the National Bus Company/Scottish Transport Group. Grants for unremunerative railway services.

1974   Railways Act
Writing off debts of the British Railways Board and introduction of freight facilities grants. 'The British Railways Board shall from 1 January 1975 operate its railway passenger system so as to provide a public service which is comparable generally with that provided by the Board at present' (directive by the Secretary of State for Transport).

1987   Channel Tunnel Act
Construction of the Channel Tunnel, but including limitations on the contribution of public moneys towards the funding of a Channel Tunnel Rail Link.

1992   Transport and Works Act
To provide a mechanism for the Secretary of State to grant statutory authority for activities which previously required private Acts of Parliament. Thus an order may provide for, amongst other things, the acquisition of land or rights over land — whether compulsorily or by agreement — for a project, the payment of compensation, incidental or ancillary works, policing and the making of bylaws.

1993   Railways Act
Separation of rail infrastructure from operations, passenger services to be provided by franchised operators, overseen by a regulatory body, rolling stock owning companies created and the general privatisation of the various aspects of the industry.

European legislation
Note that the two digit figure represents the year in which the regulation was issued.

Council Regulation 1191/69
as modified by Regulation 1893/91. Definition of scope for establishing public service requirements and the obligations of public authorities to compensate operators for carrying out public transport services.

Council Regulation 1192/69
Common rules for the normalisation of the accounts of railway undertakings.

Council Regulation 1107/70
Rules on the granting of aid for road, railways and inland waterways transport.

Council Regulation 1108/70
Introduces an accounting system for expenditure on infrastructure in respect of transport by rail, road and inland waterways.

Council Regulation 2830/77
Measures to achieve comparability between the accounting of systems and annual accounts of railway undertakings.

Council Regulation 2183/78
Lays down uniform costing principles for railway undertakings.

Commission Recommendation 922/82
Definition of a higher quality, international rail passenger transport system.

Council Directive 91/440
The development of the Community railways. Separation between the infrastructure and operations, at least in accounting terms. Management autonomy, a sound financial structure, and access to the infrastructure for combined transport and international railway groupings.

Council Directive 95/18
The licensing of railway undertakings

Council Directive 95/19
The allocation of railway infrastructure capacity and the charging of infrastructure fees.

Council Regulation 2236/95
Rules for financial contributions to Trans-European Networks, for all modes.

Omitted from this list are more general matters such as Regulations on rules for the use of the European Regional Development Fund (ERDF) or the European Social Fund (ESF). Further Directives relate to the procedures for procurement by public bodies.

Appendix 2

From the 'Objectives, Instructions and Guidance for the Franchising Director', as tabled by the Secretary of State for Transport before both Houses of Parliament on 22 March 1994.

1   'Your principal objectives are:
    — to secure that railway passenger services in Great Britain, other than exempted services, are provided under franchise agreements as soon as reasonably practicable; and
    — to secure an overall improvement in the quality of railway passenger and station services available to railway passengers.'

2   'You should also:
    — encourage efficiency and economy in the provision of railway services;
    — promote the use and cost-effective development of the railway network; and
    — promote the award of franchise agreements to companies in which qualifying railway employees ... have a substantial interest.'

3   In seeking to fulfil your objectives, make sure that franchise agreements entered into 'are consistent with the resources available to you'. Later on, the Regulator is reminded that he 'is required to have regard to your financial position'.

4   It is made clear that uniform terms of franchise agreements are not sought. 'You should leave maximum scope for the initiative of franchisees, imposing conditions no more burdensome than are required in your opinion to achieve your objectives …'

5   Open access services barely receive a mention, only to the extent that if and when it happens, 'you should take account of their existence in specifying the requirement for franchised services'.

6   Vertical franchises for both operation and infrastructure are not to be encouraged. 'Exceptionally, where for example, franchised services operate over network where no other franchise will be operating, and there seems very little prospect of other rail operators wishing to use that network, you may consider that you would secure better value for money if you proposed a degree of vertical integration…' However, Railtrack would first have to agree, and the Secretary of State would need to be consulted.

7   'For the initial letting of franchises, your specification of minimum service levels … is to be based on that being provided by BR immediately prior to franchising', allowing for seasonal changes. Service specification may include:
    — 'service frequency and capacity;
    — service availability (for example, the need for evening and weekend services);
    — provision of through services by fast trains;
    — intermediate stations served; and
    — journey time'.

    Detailed specification is seen as necessary where the franchise confers monopoly power (no example given); elsewhere, service quality requirements are seen as the means 'to ensure that the taxpayer obtains good value for money'.

8   Similarly, control of fares *levels* may require only that they be 'reasonable in all the circumstances of the case', but such provision, if made at all, is to be achieved in consultation with the Regulator.

9   For those whose journeys require the use of services of more than one franchisee, 'you are to encourage co-operation between operators to preserve and promote arrangements …' However, on ticket inter-availability, you may do so 'where you believe the benefits … will outweigh the likely benefits of price competition and service diversity.'

10 On service development, '… it will be important to ensure that service patterns do not ossify, and that operators are able to adjust services to match demand'. This clearly includes downwards as well as upwards revisions, since 'you should aim, over time, to tailor the provision of franchised services more closely to demand …' and 'you will need to develop criteria which will enable you to maximise the benefits to be obtained from their provision'. The Secretary of State must approve the criteria.

11 'Investment should be decided as far as possible by the private sector responding to passengers' requirements, but where you are making payments to secure the provision of services, rolling stock leasing companies, franchisees, Railtrack and others involved in investment will no doubt look to you for a view on future service levels.'

Appendix 3:
Passenger Service Requirement

Extract from South West Trains Ltd PSR, ASCOT–ALDERSHOT, September 1995

1   WEEKDAYS AND SATURDAYS

1.1   The service specified in paragraphs 1.2 to 1.4 below shall be provided between Ascot and Aldershot.

1.2   Service

1.2.1   The service shall call at the following stations: Ascot, Bagshot, Camberley, Frimley, Ash Vale and Aldershot.

1.2.2   An early service from Ascot shall depart at or before 0700 and an early service from Aldershot shall arrive at Ascot at or before:
(a) 0630 on a weekday; and
(b) 0700 on a Saturday.

1.2.3   A late service from Ascot shall depart at or after 0015 and a late service from Aldershot shall arrive at Ascot at or after 0000.

1.2.4   Services arriving at Ascot at or after 0700 must run through to call at all stations between Aldershot and Guildford and all departures from Ascot at or before 2300 must originate from Guildford and call at all stations between Guildford and Aldershot.

1.2.5   A minimum of two Peak services in each direction must be extended from Ascot to run through to and originate from Waterloo.

1.2.6   All other services (except those arriving at Ascot after 0000) shall connect at Ascot with services to and from Waterloo and the waiting period for such connecting services shall not exceed 10min.

1.3   Service intervals

The interval between departures from Ascot of services from Ascot and the interval between arrivals at Ascot of services from Aldershot shall be hourly in each case between the early service and the late service except that between 0700 and 0930 and between 1600 and 1900 on weekdays such intervals shall be half hourly.

1.4   Maximum Journey Time

The maximum journey time for the services shall be 32min provided that 95% of services shall have a maximum journey time of 28 min.

Part 2, Sundays, is omitted here.

The railways of Britain are facing their most uncertain period since World War 2 and the 1948 Nationalisation. Despite widespread opposition to the 1993 Railways Act, privatisation is moving on apace and the first operational franchises have passed into private ownership; the companies owning the rolling stock have been sold off and Railtrack separated from the British Railways Board.

abc National Railways is a pocket guide to the 'new' British railway scene. The author, one of the country's leading experts in public transport, describes in detail the role of the new Franchising Director, the Rail Regulator and each of the new Train Operating Units. He also examines the myriad other new companies that have emerged from the remains of BR — some involved in freight, some in catering, maintenance, and so on — and principal Acts of Parliament and European legislation, 'Objectives, Instructions and Guidance for the Franchising Director' and key extracts from the Passenger Service Requirement'.

This book will appeal to all those interested in railways, whether as a professional or an enthusiast. It is an essential and comprehensive reference to the future operations of the nation's railway network.

ISBN 0-7110-2457-X

90000

9 780711 024571

Printed in England